the Girl Guide

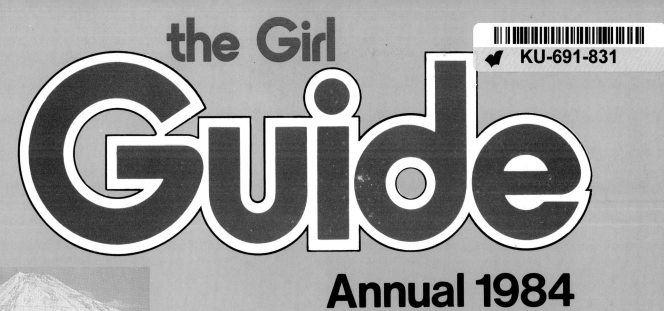

Annual 1984

edited by Penny Morris

This annual belongs to . . .

Sara McKenzie
1st Girvan
1st Ayrshire
Primrose Patrol

£2.95

BUTTERFLIES

by Vanessa Atlanta

photographs by Tony Rose

Large Skipper

Inside the glasshouse the butterflies fly about freely

I expect most of you have enjoyed watching a beautiful butterfly hovering above a flower, or basking in a patch of sunlight, but sadly such sights are becoming more and more rare. Britain's butterflies are disappearing rapidly and some varieties are almost extinct.

Butterflies thrive in areas of wild woodland and natural grassland and gradually these places are being destroyed. Grassland is being ploughed and treated with fertilisers and herbicides; mixed woodland is replaced with conifers, which shade out the undergrowth where butterflies might breed; hedges and verges around fields are removed and marsh and heathland reclaimed. All these activities destroy the butterflies' habitat.

There are, however, a growing number of people who are concerned about the fate of the butterfly, and so conservation centres have been set up so that butterflies can breed in safety. I visited one such centre – The London Butterfly House, in Syon Park – with a group of Guides, who were interested in seeing the different butterflies bred there.

In the British Isles there are some 69 species of butterfly. This may seem a lot, but there are over 700 species in Europe, and more than 100,000 worldwide. Our climate is very hard on butterflies, so we have very few indigenous species. Weather conditions can greatly influence the number of butterflies in any year. A hard winter and cold spring affects the eggs which were laid the previous autumn, and are due to hatch in

Meadow Brown

April or in May. During a sunless summer, fewer eggs are laid as the females lay only in bright weather.

All our indigenous species hibernate, some as butterflies, but most as either eggs, larvae, or pupae. The Small Tortoiseshell is one of the commonest British butterflies. The adults hibernate through the winter and in the spring the female awakes and finds a suitable place to lay her eggs. She may lay up to a hundred eggs, usually on a stinging nettle. The caterpillars hatch after about two weeks, and cover themselves with a fine web of silk. Beneath this, they concentrate on feeding. As they grow they gradually dispense with the silk and start to go their own ways, until three to four weeks later they are ready to spin a cocoon. The chrysalis stage takes about ten to fourteen days, during which the pupa is changing into a butterfly. This transformation is called metamorphosis.

The name pupa is derived from the latin word for a doll, and at this stage the creature appears to be wrapped in swaddling clothes, rather like a miniature Egyptian mummy. The adult butterfly, or imago, emerges in darkness, its wings flat and crumpled. Once it has hauled itself out it begins to pump blood into a network of veins within its 'baggy' wings. The wings gradually expand and after about half an hour are fully extended. The imago then draws the blood back into its body and the veins harden into a rigid framework.

The butterfly holds its wings up together until they are extended

Ringlet

Common Blue (underside)

Holly Blue

Common Blue (upperside)

Green-veined White

5

This glass case houses mounted butterflies from all over the world

Small Copper

Left: the Owl Butterfly.
Can you think why it is so named?

Comma

and only then, when they are quite rigid, does it open them out and allow the sun to dry them off.

Once it is ready to fly, the butterfly has just one objective – to find a mate. Feeding is necessary only to provide energy, as the butterfly does not grow any more.

What can you do to help?

One of the most important things you can do is to make more people aware of the need to conserve the butterflies' natural habitation.

If you can, try to persuade people with gardens to plant a few of the flowers that are particularly attractive to butterflies. The following plants all provide food for adult butterflies: Aubretia, Buddleia, Catmint, Cornflowers, Golden Rod, Honesty, Lavender, Michaelmas Daisy, Phlox, Sweet William, Verbena, Wallflowers.

Butterflies also need plants to lay their eggs on. It may be more difficult to persuade people to leave a patch of nettles in their garden, but a small area of wild flowers and weeds will provide a breeding ground for several of our butterflies.

The Small Tortoiseshell and Peacock butterflies both like to lay their eggs on nettles; other butterflies will lay on coarse grass, sorrel, clover, dock and brambles.

Another way you can help is to keep an eye on any wild places

Right: Butterflies love buddleia

6

near your home, and if they seem endangered, for example through the dumping of rubbish, contact your local Nature Conservation Trust and see if you can form a task force to protect the area. Butterflies are one of the first creatures to suffer from such hazards as pollution, so if you are helping to conserve the butterflies' habitat, other creatures will benefit too.

There are several organisations you could contact for information about butterfly conservation:

The British Butterfly
Conservation Society,
Tudor House,
Quorn,
Leicestershire LE12 8AD

The Nature Conservancy Council,
19–20 Belgrave Square,
London SW1X 8PY

The Royal Society for Nature
Conservation,
The Green,
Nettleham,
Lincolnshire

The World Wildlife Fund,
29 Greville Street,
London EC1N 8AX

Why not take the Conservation Badge? By joining a group or

society who work for conservation and taking part in a project of theirs, you can fulfil clause 3, or you could cultivate a small piece of land, planting wild plants obtained through the Nature Conservancy Council. In conserving plants that provide food for caterpillars and butterflies you will be helping to conserve insect life too.

Small Tortoiseshell

The magnificent Red Admiral, now sadly a rare sight, and (below) a Peacock butterfly, still fairly common

The Guides were able to watch these two butterflies from close quarters, probably examples of Heliconius Melpomone from S. Africa pictured below

7

EXTRA-QUICK KNIT

This sweater is easy and quick to knit because it is made on extra-large needles.

You need a maximum of 7 40 gm balls of Mohair No 1 Double Knitting, or a mohair and acrylic mix. The sweater in the picture was knitted in Patricia Roberts' 'Woolly Bear'.

Also 1 pair No 7 (4½ mm)
        1 pair No 000
knitting needles.

Now you must measure to find your length for the body and sleeves. Ask someone to help you measure from collar to hip bone down your back and from armpit to wrist. Make a note of these measurements. Alternatively, you could measure a jumper that fits you comfortably.

Abbreviations K knit; p purl; st(s) stitch(es); st st stocking stitch (1 row knit, 1 row purl); reversed st st reversed stocking stitch (1 row purl, 1 row knit); patt pattern.

Stitches used

a) K2, p2 rib on No 7 needles
1st row K3, *p2, K2, repeat from * to last st, K1
2nd row K1, *p2, K2, repeat from * to last 3 sts, p2, K1
These 2 rows form the K2, p2 rib

b) Pattern on No 000 needles
Work 4 rows in st st then 2 rows in reversed st st
i.e. 1st row knit
        2nd row purl
        3rd row knit
        4th row purl
        5th row purl

6th row knit
These 6 rows form the pattern.

The Back
Using No 7 (4½ mm) needles cast on 60 sts and work in K2, p2 rib until work measures 2½ ins/6 cms, ending on the wrong side, decreasing 10 sts evenly along the last row, to leave 50 sts.
Change to No 000 needles and proceed in patt until the work equals your back measurement, ending on the wrong side. Cast off loosely.

The Front
Work exactly as for the back but stop when the work measures 3 ins/8 cms *less* than the back, ending on the wrong side.

Shape neck
Next row patt for 21 sts, cast off 8 sts loosely, patt for 21 sts.
Working on the first 21 sts only proceed as follows:
1st row patt to end
2nd row cast off 2 sts, patt to end
Repeat 1st and 2nd rows, leaving 17 sts. Continue without further shaping until work measures same as the back, ending on the wrong side. Cast off loosely.

With wrong side facing, rejoin yarn to remaining 21 sts and proceed as follows:
1st row patt to end
2nd row patt to end
3rd row cast off 2 sts, patt to end

Repeat 2nd and 3rd rows, leaving 17 sts. Continue without further shaping until work measures same as the back, ending on the wrong side. Cast off loosely.

The Sleeves (both alike)
Using No 7 (4½ mm) needles cast on 36 sts and work in K2, p2 rib until work measures 3 ins/8 cms, ending on wrong side, decreasing 8 sts evenly along the last row, to leave 28 sts.
Change to No 000 needles and proceed in patt until work measures 1 in/3 cms *less* than your arm measurement.
Next row increase by 7 sts evenly along the row to give 35 sts. Continue in patt until work equals your arm measurement, ending on the wrong side. Cast off loosely.
Repeat for second sleeve.

The Neckband
Using No 7 (4½ mm) needles cast on 76 sts, then work in K2, p2 rib until work measures 1 in/3 cms, ending on right side. Cast off loosely.

To Make Up
Sew up the side seams of the body, leaving an opening 7½ ins/19 cms for sleeves. Sew up the shoulder seams. Sew in the neckband, taking care to space it evenly, and joining the two ends at centre back. Sew up the sleeve seams. Sew in the sleeves.

CROSSWORD

by Phil Stuart

ACROSS

1 Boil gently (6)
6 Sad (7)
8 Deeds (7)
11 Young geese (8)
15 Girl's name (4)
17 Type of cake (3)
18 To see with (4)
19 Finish (3)
20 Fish (4)
21 Disastrous (7)
23 Throw (5)
26 Functioning (2)
28 Group of eight (5)
32 Alien (7)
34 Tax (4)
35 Green vegetable (3)
36 Excuse (4)
37 Horse (3)
38 Building support (4)
39 Loot (8)
44 Eternally (7)
45 Glad (7)
46 Avenue (6)

DOWN

2 Lichen (4)
3 Shower (4)
4 Pastry dish (3)
5 Demands (7)
7 Limb (3)
9 Waterway (5)
10 Come into by death (7)
12 Scandinavian man's name (4)
13 Small island (5)
14 Vend (4)
16 Photographic device (4)
17 Swelling (7)
22 Strolling (7)
24 Revising (7)
25 Clergyman (abbrev.) (3)
27 Press, tv. etc. (5)
29 Wash (5)
30 Rip (4)
31 Tempest (7)
32 Action (4)
33 Close (4)
40 Hearing organs (4)
41 Impulse (4)
42 Ocean (3)
43 Animal doctor (3)

Solution on page 63

SCRAMBLED BADGES

by Ann Martin

If you unscramble the phrases below you will find the names of some Ranger Interest Certificates that you could work for when you join Rangers.

Example: Will King Hal – Hillwalking
Now try these –

Roast shies

Hear cry

Tis rat

Star on Rome

A clear lombrond

Amard

Wait on bas

C tramp caf

Wingcer

Exorprel

Rare Ranger wolf

Heat Megan Momen

Come in hot Marc

Kind Veris

Right Whips

Carpet slave

Solution on page 57

Nursing-a caring career

Have you ever thought you'd like to be a nurse? A great many girls, and boys too, are drawn towards nursing as it offers the satisfaction of knowing that what you are doing really helps others.

Many people think that nursing begins and ends in the hospital ward but in fact the profession extends through the entire community; from the district nurse, or community health worker, to those nurses involved in research work; from nursing mentally handicapped people to caring for newborn babies.

But inevitably when most young people first think of nursing as a career, they think of general nursing in a hospital. A hospital nurse works as part of a team which includes physiotherapists, occupational therapists and dietitians, but it is the nurse who is responsible for the day to day care of the patient and is expected to notice changes in the patient's condition, as *she* knows the patient best.

Nursing is becoming more technical nowadays with the development of heart and nerve surgery, and transplant surgery. Some patients may for a time be dependent on life-maintaining equipment, and the nurse has to understand and manage this. Training has to cover many subjects, both in theory and practice, including physiology, anatomy, sociology and psychology.

Most nurses are trained in district general hospitals. I went to St Thomas's Hospital to talk to the head of admissions at the Nightingale School and some of the student nurses there.

Each nursing school has its own educational requirements; St Thomas's prefers students who have A levels. Some hospitals ask for passes in particular subjects so anyone considering nursing should check that they are studying for the right exams.

More generally, one of the most important requirements is good health. Nurses need to be fit and strong as the work is so physically demanding.

Anyone who has done any voluntary work, for example helping with old people, will find this taken into consideration by the selectors and I was told that applicants with relevant Guide badges, such as First Aid, Home Nurse, Child Care, should mention this on the application form as it is taken as an indication of their interest in caring for others.

Hobbies are considered too, as they give the selection panel an idea of the candidate as a whole person, whether they are a loner or prefer groups, and whether they work well alone, or better as part of a team. Outside interests are important to anyone with such a demanding job to help them relax after a busy day.

Most nursing schools don't take students under the age of eighteen, so anyone leaving school after O levels has time to fill in before starting their training.

Like most nursing schools, St Thomas's has a long waiting list. The students I spoke to had been offered places at the Nightingale School in October 1980 but didn't begin training until March 1982. Caroline, who was eighteen, spent the time working in a psychiatric hospital, Barbara (nineteen) worked in Paris, Bernadette (nineteen) helped to care for terminally ill patients in a hospice, and Paula (nineteen) did a secretarial course.

I was interested to discover that Caroline, Barbara and Bernadette all had close relatives who were nurses, and the admissions officer agreed that nursing and medicine do seem to run in families. Of the four girls, Caroline was the only one who had seriously considered any other career apart from nursing – the other three had wanted to nurse for as long as they could remember.

I asked whether there was anything that particularly worried them before they began training. Paula had been concerned about the amount of responsibility they would be given, but soon learnt that the student nurses were never left to cope in any situation beyond their capabilities, and were given responsibility very gradually.

Once at the school, the first thing new nurses are taught is how to look after themselves, as many of them have not lived away from home before. It is essential that they keep themselves healthy and eat well. The four I talked to were all living in the Nurses Home and agreed that this was best for the first six months, until they'd settled in and made some friends.

I wondered whether there was anything about the training so far that they hadn't anticipated, and all four groaned and laughed – they hadn't realised that they would be expected to study so hard. The first two weeks had been spent in college every day from 9.00 till 3.30 and they were given plenty of homework. In the third week they were allowed onto the wards to do general observation, watching procedures and seeing how the wards are run. Then it was back to the classroom again.

The first part of the course concentrates on basic patient care but later the students would be spending eight weeks on medical wards and eight weeks on surgical wards. They were all looking forward to this as it would be their first chance to get to know any patients. Once on the wards they would have to start shift work, but in the first six months they would only have to do two night duties, on observation.

Obviously some aspects of patient care cannot be taught in the classroom. I asked whether there was anything in particular that worried them. Barbara had been rather worried about giving an injection for the first time, but said that when they were taught this they practised on oranges, not patients!

I finished by asking whether they'd thought about what to do after they qualified: All four had quite definite ideas: Bernadette wanted to study midwifery, Caroline wanted to nurse sick children, and Paula and Barbara both wanted to work abroad, perhaps doing V.S.O. Barbara's sister was working in an eye clinic in Africa and this sort of work appealed to both girls.

Anyone who is thinking of applying to train as a nurse should consider very carefully just what is involved. Applicants do sometimes forget about the unpleasant aspects of the job. One girl dropped out of the course at St Thomas's when she realised she couldn't bear to touch people. But the selection procedure is fairly rigorous and unsuitable candidates are usually spotted and turned down.

If you are interested in nursing as a career, you can write to, or call at, the Nursing and Health Services Careers Centre, 121–123 Edgware Road, London W2 2HX, for more information.

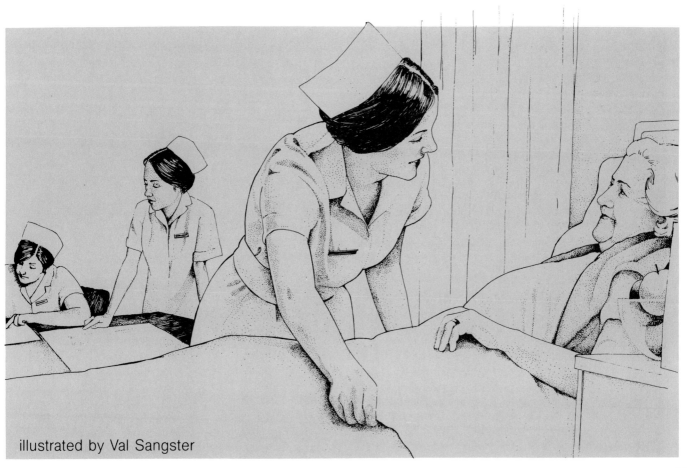

illustrated by Val Sangster

by Agnes Szudek

illustrations by Viv Quillin

Clementine Hall and her mother came out of the school bazaar laden with packages and waited at the bus stop.

"I'll never understand it," Mrs Hall sighed, shaking her head. "It's always the same, this bazaaring business. We get rid of our junk and bring home other people's. Next year, we'll go to the pictures instead."

She was carrying an old rectangular bread bin, some pieces of cutlery tied with string, a lace dress and a black violin case, worn white round the edges.

Clementine clutched a roll of dog-eared comics which she had bought for five pence, some padded coat-hangers and a brown Victorian hat-rack that stuck out at all angles. "Well, you didn't *have* to buy anything, Mum. Nobody asked you to," ventured Clementine. Her words sounded a fraction less than polite so she added an exaggerated grin, to keep the peace.

"They give you looks with their bogey eyes, if you don't buy something," her mother said, pausing first to accept the grin.

"Beady eyes."

"That's what I said." Mrs Hall waved down an on-coming bus and they climbed aboard. She went on complaining about bazaars as they settled themselves on the seat.

They had recently come to live in town so that Mr Hall could be nearer his work at the Foot-Rest Carpet Factory Ltd, but Mrs Hall was not happy at the top of a tower block.

"I'd rather be back in the countryside where I was born," she grumbled, spreading her complaints further afield.

"Oh Mum! We could be, any minute!" Clementine gasped. "We're on the wrong bus. There shouldn't be an S bend. We've never passed one before. That was an S bend. It said so."

Mrs Hall leapt to her feet and was in the gangway, then on the other side of the bus within seconds, flattening passengers with her paraphenalia.

"Ring the bell! It's the wrong bus! We've got to get off!" she called in panic.

The conductor obliged and the bus lurched to a halt at the next stop. Clementine, her mother, and their goods, found themselves on the pavement in what seemed to be a strange part of town.

Mrs Hall was flustered. "Oh dear! We should have reconnoitred the district when we moved here. I'm lost!"

"Cheer up, Mum," Clementine said, squeezing her mother's arm. "We'll make it, with a bit of luck. Let's catch a bus across the road and go back to where we started."

"Another bus? And get lost somewhere else? Not likely! It's Shank's pony for us, my girl. We've got four good feet between us," declared Mrs Hall, stepping out like an infantryman.

Clementine checked her feet, crossed her eyes and strode on behind her mother. They negotiated the S bend like a short snake, but Mrs Hall was not cut out to be an infantryman. She was soon out of breath and sat down on a garden wall to recover.

"Oh, my blood pressure! It's further than I thought," she puffed. "Take the weight off your feet for a minute, Clemmy."

But Clementine did not sit down. She was staring at a notice in the garden, behind the wall.

"Hey, Crescendo Pink!" she shouted excitedly. "Crescendo Pink! Look!"

"Quick! Cover your head!" uttered her mother, covering hers with an empty string bag – the only thing she had available. "What is it? What is it?"

"It's all right, Mum. It's a music teacher," said Clementine, falling about with laughter. "It says so, there." She read the words on the notice.

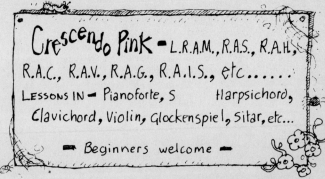

"A piano teacher, Mum! I've always wanted to learn the piano, haven't I? Could I have piano lessons? Pl-pl-pl-please?" Clementine begged, kneeling on the pavement.

"Don't be silly, child. Get up! We haven't got a piano." Her mother twisted round to look at the sign, crushing a cluster of shady begonias in a box. "You never mentioned the word 'piano' when we lived in the country. You could have had one then. We'd plenty of space." Mrs Hall sounded as though she was speaking of a large pet.

"We could buy one. They're often advertised for sale in the paper," Clementine said persuasively.

"You can't keep dogs or pianos in a multi-storey carpark."

"Flat, Mum, flat. We could try. I don't want a dog."

"Out of the question." Mrs Hall humped herself off the wall. "But we've got a perfectly good violin now, so we'll put it to some use. Then I won't feel so bad about bazaaring."

"But Mum, I don't want to learn – couldn't we come back next year? I mean, we've got all this stuff with us now."

Clementine had no wish to learn the violin, but her mother was already pushing open the wooden gate, so she tried to conceal the cumbersome hat-rack under her arm, and followed her down the path. The pegs stuck upwards and outwards in various directions and refused to be concealed. Her mother still had the string bag on her head, but before Clementine could tell her, the front door of the large grey house opened, and an arpeggio floated out into the garden: 'Doh - me - soh - doh - soh - me - doh!'

The trilling in perfect pitch was followed by a tall angular lady with ringlets, dark-rimmed spectacles and a long, colourful patchwork skirt. In one hand she held a tuning-fork.

"Oh," she said, drawing back at the sight of Clementine. "I'm afraid I don't teach the bagpipes."

"It's not. It's a hat-rack," Clementine explained.

"Sorry, I don't teach the hat-rack either," said the tall lady, airily. "You'll have to try someone else."

But Mrs Hall was in a determined mood. "Please be so kind as to give us a minute. It's true we're not a very musical family – tone-deaf to be honest – but my Clementine's got good long fingers and we've just bought this violin at the school bazaar," she said, depositing her purchases on the doorstep and opening the violin case like a travelling saleswoman.

But Miss Pink was not interested in looking at the instrument.

"A beginner on violin, from school bazaar. Is that so? Let me see."

She pulled up a handful of skirt and looked closely at one of the patchwork squares. "Yes, I'm free on Fridays at six – except when it's Friday the thirteenth. I *never* teach on Friday the thirteenth. It's more than my musical genius is worth. Other Fridays – yes. Will that suit?"

"Oh, nicely, thanks ever so," said Mrs Hall. "I'll see she's here on the dot with clean hands and everything."

Crescendo Pink let her skirt fall back into place by releasing it with a precise flick of her left thumb and forefinger.

It was then that Clementine noticed much more writing on the patchwork pieces, as though the skirt was used as a memo pad. Miss Pink struck her tuning-fork on the hat-rack and repeated the perfect A. *"Friday at si-i-ix! Friday at si-i-ix!"* she intoned, swung round with a flutter of skirts and went back into the house.

"Odd sort of bird," Mrs Hall remarked. "Brilliant, I expect. Have you noticed, all brilliant people are odd-bods? She's got to be something with a name like that. You'll be in good hands, Clemmy, I bet, but my feet are killing me. We'll take a bus home, like you said."

They crossed the road and after closely interrogating the crew of the first bus that came along, Mrs Hall and her daughter climbed aboard. Within minutes, they caught sight of the tall concrete slabs of their own tower block.

When Friday evening came, Clementine went reluctantly to her first music lesson. As she took the violin from its case, Crescendo Pink almost fell upon it in delirium.

"But it's a Rarivarius!" she shrieked, rushing to examine it by the window. "Do you know you've got a Rarivarius, dear thing?"

"Yes," replied Clementine. She knew that much because it was written on it.

"But where did you get it?"

"The school bazaar for fifty-nine pence, like Mum said."

"No, no, no, you couldn't have. Not a Rarivarius. Why, I'd given up all hope of ever holding one of these in my arms." Crescendo Pink cuddled the instrument like a baby. "My dear thing, I've scoured the world, even been to Nepal where one was said to be sighted," she jabbered on.

"Don't you mean a yeti?" Clementine asked her, used to her mother making mistakes.

"Not at all. A musical sherpa played something. But it turned out to be a violin he'd made himself, excellent in its own way, of course. However, now to work. I'm all a-tingle at the very sight of this exquisite darling. With such a gem, I'll teach you to play like Yehudi Menuhin. Now there's a promise!"

Clementine had no hope that she could help Miss Pink to keep such a promise, but from that moment she was treated like a star pupil. First, Crescendo Pink showed her how to stand, where to put her chin, how to hold the bow, and the names of the four strings: E, A, D and G. The rest of the lesson was taken up with her teacher playing the Rarivarius in spectacular style. Her ringlets jumped about like springs; her head darted from left to right as though it was going to swing off; her eyes were tightly shut; her breath came in loud ecstatic gasps, and she made the sweetest music that Clementine had ever heard.

At the end of thirty minutes, she still could not bear to be parted from the treasured violin and accompanied Clementine as far as the bus stop, surprising the neighbourhood with the strains of Brahms's Symphony No 2 in D major.

When she got home, Clementine's mother and father had already started dinner. "Mum! Dad! I've got a Rarivarius! Miss Pink says so," she cried, bursting through the door.

"Very likely!" said her father, thinking she said 'a Stradivarius'.

"A Disprin-gargle and a hot-water-bottle should help," said her mother, thinking she said 'a rare virus'. "It must have something to do with the weather and all these secret experiments somewhere or other. Sit down and have your dinner first."

They were both pleased to tell the neighbours that they had a musician in the family at last. But although Clementine worked hard at it, practising every evening after school, she did not improve at the violin. She reached *Twinkle, Twinkle, Little Star* on page eleven of her book, and there she stuck. Her chin wouldn't stay on the chin rest and the notes were all wrong. Her father said that one stroke sounded like a cat wailing, two strokes sounded like two cats wailing, and a scale needed to have a boot thrown at it!

"You want to try some dubbin on that bow," grumbled her father one evening when he could bear it no longer.

"But dubbin's for football boots, Dad," said Clementine, almost in tears. "Anyway, I'd rather learn the piano – or even football, for that matter."

"Come on, you know what I mean – the stuff you should put on a bow." Her father lapsed into silence after blocking his ears with cottonwool.

"There now, you've upset her, Wally. Never mind, Clemmy, I think you're doing very well, considering," said her mother who, of course, came from a tone-deaf family.

Clementine, deeply offended by the cottonwool, took the violin to her bedroom. She closed the door and threw the case on her bed.

"I don't want to learn the stupid thing anyway. I want a piano," she said, defiantly. But as the case hit the bed, it bounced before it came to rest, and in that bounce there was a rattle. The violin and bow were in her hand, so what had rattled? Then she remembered there was a small flap inside the case. She had tried to draw Miss Pink's attention to it because although she knew nothing about violins, she could see the flap should open.

Kneeling on the floor beside her bed, she sniffed round the edges of the crescent-shaped flap. It was stuck with something that smelt like candlewax, probably from long ago before the days of electricity, she thought. Taking a nail file from her dressing-table, she scraped away at the wax until most of it had flaked off.

The flap came up without any difficulty. Inside was a round ivory box with a horse's head carved on the top. And inside the box was a block of amber-coloured rosin for the bow.

"Dubbin, says Dad," snorted Clementine. "I'll give it another go." She stroked the bow with the rosin, as she had seen her teacher do and tried *Twinkle,*

Twinkle, Little Star once again.

As she played, she felt a tingling sensation running along her right arm. It travelled across the top of her head and down her left arm until she felt as though she was bursting with violin energy – just like Crescendo Pink.

She played the piece over and over without a single mistake: *lento, presto, forte, piano,* with the bow and *pizzicato*. She played while she danced about the room feeling like a professional musician to the tips of her toes. Her breath came loudly like Crescendo Pink's and her head bobbed about in time, pigtails flying.

She did not hear her bedroom door open slowly, nor see her astonished parents looking in. She danced and played on in a frenzy, until her mother said, "I told you she was doing nicely, didn't I, Wally? But enough's enough, Clemmy. You'd better pop into bed with that rare virus. It could get worse."

The tingling was still in her arms and legs as Clementine fell asleep the moment her head touched the pillow. She tossed and turned in a terrible dream about bowing her violin with football boots.

The following Friday, when Crescendo Pink heard the new musical Clementine, she clapped her hands together, raised her left leg and caught hold of the hem of her patchwork skirt.

"You've just beaten the deadline for the 'Infant Phenomenon'," she announced. "Yes, this is my week for testing your true colours as a serious musician. I've got it all marked here on the polka dots. Congratulations! You'll be playing at the Albert Hall before you're much older. I'm thrilled with your amazing progress!"

continued on page 26

HERE'S HOW YOU SPELL
LEXIGRAM

Devised by Cecilia Fellner

Are you always being told you must improve your spelling? An awful lot of quite clever people never manage to learn to spell with confidence. They keep having to consult a dictionary – that interrupts their train of thought – and sometimes they can't remember what they'd intended to write in the first place.

Here's a sort of game you can play which will help you remember how to spell words you find particularly difficult.

First of all, SEPARATE – or is it SEPERATE? Do both look equally right, or perhaps equally wrong, to you? This is when you need to construct a lexigram.

a) be sure you have the correct spelling – in this case SEPARATE

b) think of the meaning of the word

c) think of an appropriate word which you do know how to spell and which contains in it the correct version of the spelling you want to remember. In this case, the best word I can think of is PARTS

d) write down the sequence of three letters these two words have in common in very large capitals, so that they can be shared

e) attach the other letters in smaller capitals

SE**PAR**ATE
TS

Take a good long look at what you have done and I am sure you will never forget how to spell SEPARATE.

Remember, to EXA**GGER**ATE a problem is
to make it BI**GGER** than it is!

Do you always remember the 'c' in ascend and descend?
How about:

He D**ESC**ENDED
the **ESC**ALATOR

And this one, a two-in-one:

A B**EA**CH of sand
lies by the S**EA** A long way from
The old TR**EE**CH BEECH

Here's another:

It's A**POL**ITE and wise
to A**POL**OGIZE

No need to apologize for your spelling now!

15

BAKE ME A CAKE

by Doreen Forni

The cakes I am going to tell you how to make have one basic recipe. By adding extra ingredients you can make a variety of different cakes. The recipe is very quick and easy.

BASIC SANDWICH CAKE

2 6″ shallow cake tins
100g/4oz self-raising flour
pinch of salt
100g/4 oz caster sugar
100g/4 oz soft margarine
2 eggs (size 3 or 4)
1 level tsp baking powder
4 drops vanilla essence

1 Light the oven at gas regulo 4/350°F/180°C.
2 Cut two circles of greaseproof paper to fit the bottoms of two sandwich cake tins. Put the lining paper in and lightly grease it.
3 Put all the ingredients into a large mixing bowl, adding the eggs separately by breaking them into a cup first.
4 Stir everything together with a wooden spoon, beating harder as it mixes, until it is smooth and creamy, and there are no lumps of margarine.
5 Scrape the wooden spoon clean then, using a tablespoon and knife, put half the mixture into each tin, smoothing it with the knife.
6 Place the tins on the middle shelf of the oven for 20–25 minutes. Remove when the cake is firm to touch and just beginning to shrink from the sides of the tin.
7 Carefully turn the cakes out onto a cooling tray, easing round the edges of the tin with a knife first. Peel off the paper and leave the cakes to cool.

VARIATIONS

Chocolate Sandwich Cake

Substitute 25g/1 oz self-raising flour with 25g/1 oz cocoa, then make as for the basic recipe. Sieve the cocoa as it is sometimes lumpy.

Lemon or Orange Cake

Grate the rind or zest of a lemon or orange into the basic mixture using a fine grater. Make sure you do not grate in any of the white pith under the skin as this is bitter. Then cut the fruit in half and squeeze out the juice. Add 1 dessertspoonful of the juice to the cake mixture before stirring it. Keep the rest of the juice to flavour the filling or icing.

Spice Cake

Add two teaspoons of mixed spice to the basic recipe. This cake is also good with orange flavouring, either add rind and juice to the spice cake or decorate it with orange-flavoured icing or butter cream.

Chocolate Chip Cake

Follow the basic recipe and add 100g/4 oz of polka dots or small pieces of cooking chocolate to the mixture. These pieces of chocolate stay whole while the cake is baking. If you prefer, you can put this mixture into a deeper cake tin, instead of using shallow tins. Cook it for 35–40 minutes if you do this, and check it is baked by putting a clean skewer into the centre of the cake. If the skewer comes out clean the cake is ready.

Apple Cake

Add 1 teaspoon of mixed spice to the basic mixture. Peel, core and slice two eating apples, then stir the pieces into the beaten mixture, along with about 50g/2oz of sultanas.

All these cakes can be made larger by doubling the ingredients, or by adding 50g/2oz more of each dry ingredient, one more egg, and another ½tsp of baking powder. However, if you make a larger chocolate cake, still only replace 25g/1oz of the flour with cocoa.

FILLINGS

Jam Spread a layer of strawberry or raspberry jam between the sponges.

Butter cream Beat together 50 g/2 oz butter or magarine with 75 g/3 oz caster or icing sugar. When the mixture looks pale and creamy it is ready to spread on the sponge. You can use this to sandwich the two sponges together, and also spread it on the top of the cake. Mark it with a fork and decorate it with grated chocolate.

You can also flavour the butter cream with orange or lemon juice, or drinking chocolate (1tsp) depending on the type of cake you have made. (It is best not to use cocoa powder in this as it has a raw taste.)

TOPPINGS

Butter cream as mentioned above.

Melted chocolate Break 100 g/4 oz cooking chocolate onto a metal plate and put the plate over a pan of hot, *not* boiling, water. When the chocolate has melted, use a round-bladed knife to spread it over the top of the cake. Decorate it with some grated chocolate flakes.

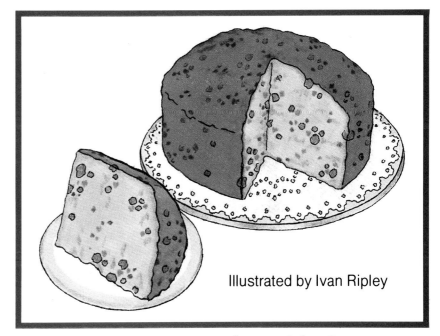

Illustrated by Ivan Ripley

Icing Measure 6 tbsp sifted icing sugar into a bowl, then add 3/4 tsps of orange or lemon juice. Stir until smooth, then spread onto the top of an orange or lemon cake. Smooth it with a warmed knife (hold the blade under the hot tap for a minute).

Use bought orange or lemon slices to decorate white icing.

If you want to use coloured icing, add liquid colouring, but be very careful and only add a drop at a time, as a little goes a long way and bright red cake does not look very appetising!

All the above toppings can be decorated by marking with a fork. You can also use chocolate drops, buttons or Smarties if you like.

A special cake
How about making a special fruit cake using the same method? Use it as a birthday cake or even for Christmas.

ALL-IN-ONE FRUIT CAKE

7″ deep cake tin
225 g/8 oz self-raising flour
10 ml/2 level tsps mixed spice
5 ml/1 level tsp baking powder
100 g/4 oz tub margarine
100 g/4 oz soft brown sugar
225 g/8 oz dried fruit
2 eggs
about 30 ml/2 tbsp milk

1 Light the oven at gas regulo 3/325°F/170°C.
2 Line the base of the cake tin with a circle of greaseproof paper, then lightly grease the paper and the sides of the tin.
3 Put all the ingredients except the milk into a large mixing bowl, and beat them together until smooth, adding the milk once the other ingredients have combined.
4 Put the mixture into the tin and bake it for about 1 hour 45 minutes. Test the cake by putting a clean skewer into the centre. If it comes out clean the cake is ready. If the skewer has cake mix on it, pop it back into the oven for another 10 minutes, then re-test.
5 When the cake is ready, let it cool for a minute in the tin, then loosen it round the edge with a knife and turn it out onto a cooling tray.

Start the day the best possible way! A brisk run along the beach! Your track-suit is the best thing to wear to the beach anyway – it keeps you warm at the end of the day when the sun's gone in.

Choose your sunglasses carefully. Make sure they're comfortable (or you won't wear them) and that they're the best quality you can afford – cheap sunglasses do not scre out rays that could damage your eyes.

Prepare a beauty bag. Take a bottle of water to ri the salt from your face and hair, a tin of refreshi cleansing pads, lipgloss or vaseline, tissues, a hairbrush or comb and suncream. Elastoplast often comes in handy too!

Do take care when sunbathing. Remember that the rays get through c and that you'll tan (or burn) quicker in the water, so apply sunscreen at frec intervals. Start off with a high protection cream if you've not been in the sun then change to a lower protection cream when you're a little tanned. Use an after-sun lotion at the end of the day to keep your tan longer.

Make a nose-shield with coloured paper or card. A red, peeling nose isn't chic – a bright pink nose-shield is!

If you're unlucky enough to burn, you have to use calamine lotion. It isn't pretty but it will stop the hurting! Don't let it happen again!

BEAUTY ON THE BEACH

Wear a flower in your hair! Wear lip-gloss or vaseline <u>always</u> in the sun.

Keep your hair off your face when sunbathing. Hair that's sticky with salt water and wind can be slicked down with a setting gel, then twisted into little knots with hair-pins.

Take a giant American sandwich with you. Layer crisply fried bacon, lettuce, tuna, cheese, egg, anchovies in four or five slices of bread. Follow it with fruit or 'Chinese Chews' – mix together 2oz. chopped walnuts, 8oz. chopped dates, 4oz. S.R. flour, 2 eggs, 8oz. sugar. Bake in greased swiss roll tin for 20mins, at 400°F. Cut into fingers and roll in icing sugar.

Take a bottle of lemonade, plastic glasses and straws and buy a scoop of ice-cream to make an ice-cream sundae.

Show a beautiful back! Make a scrub with equal proportions of ground, dried orange peel, ground almonds and oatmeal. Mix them together and scrub your body at bath-time.

Continue your beautiful skin routine with a sea-weed scrub — most refreshing!

FASHION

You'll want to carry a minimum, so think very carefully about what you'll need during a day on the beach.

A cotton shawl is very useful – it can go around your shoulders or be worn around your waist as a skirt.

Or take a kanga – the nicest ones are African, but you can cut a length of pretty fabric to the right size (110 cm. × 145 cm.) and use that. There are numerous ways of wearing a kanga – here are three, but experiment!

Buy a few box of pretty beads make lots of sim necklaces. Knot larger beads thin s or velvet ribbon:

① Bring corners to the centre front and simply knot and roll over the top edge to secure.

② Hold kanga up in front of you, knot the cor at the centre back and pull kanga through your legs to your waist at the back, cross corners and bring them around, to knot at centre front waist.

③ Hold one corner over right shoulder drape kanga around your body to the other corner at centre back. Ma sure that the kanga is draped at e angle to your body.

Real kanga experts carry all their beach essential is them too! Simply knot all four corners together and slip over your shoulder.

THE BEACH

Take a lovely lunch—cut a melon in half, scoop out and chop the flesh and mix it with chopped tomatoes, black grapes, a little mint and french dressing.

Take a bottle of apple juice and a peach each—slice the peach into the juice, drink the juice and eat the peach!

a pretty, lacy handkerchief alf and sew it across the t of a simple camisole.

y-up your swimsuits—
ad beads onto your
ni straps, knot
e beads onto thin
n and tie it round
ides of the pants
longer leg look.
tiny fake flowers
a bikini, or rows of
ac braid diagonally
s a plain swimsuit.
stripes of coloured
on to emphasise the
s of your swimsuit.

A man's string vest, dyed a pretty colour with cold water dye looks stunning over your swimsuit.
Dye your espadrilles to match.

ghten up your plimsolls—stick rows of bright coloured on down the side, and use ribbon as a lace. Or dye Dylon Shoe Dye and add contrasting fringing.

End the day as you began, with a run along the beach!

TIE-BREAK

A game for two players – you need two dice, a shaker and one round counter (the ball).

SERVING The first server places the counter behind the baseline in any one of the three circles on her righthand side **before** throwing the two dice. Her opponent serves the next two points from her side of the net, after which the first server serves the fourth and fifth points, and so on. After serving from the right side, serve next from the left.

PLAYING Throw the two dice and add their values together.* Make as many moves across the net, over and back, as this number allows. If the sequence of circles you have chosen ends before the number is reached you will have to stop sooner.

*Exceptions: if you throw a double one it counts as a double fault and you lose the point;
              if you throw a double six it counts as an ace, you win the point immediately.

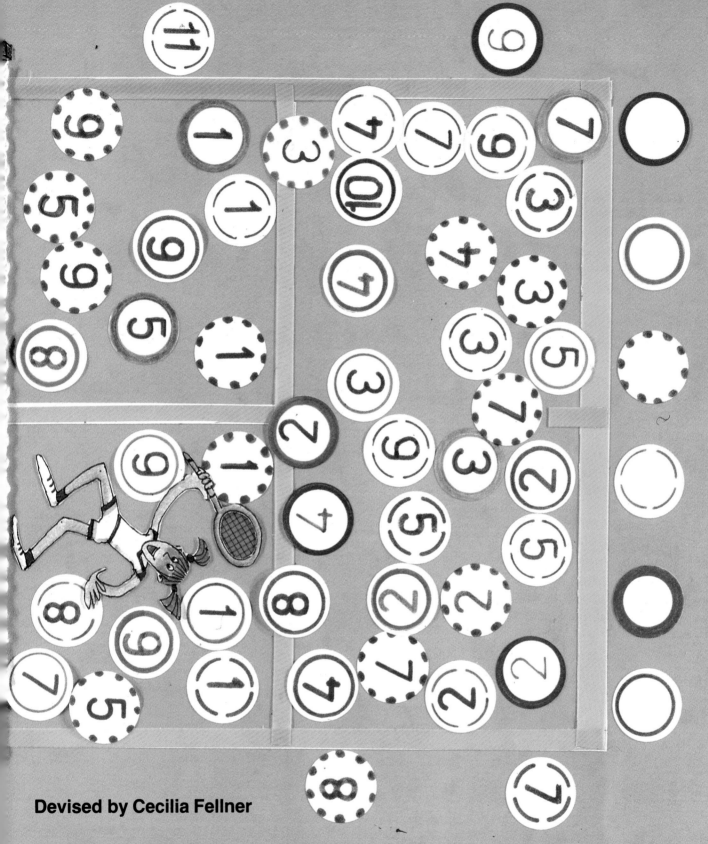

Devised by Cecilia Fellner

SCORING   If the ball ends **in court** on the **opposite** side of the net from the server, the **server wins** the point.

If the ball ends **out of court** on the **opposite** side of the net from the server, the **server loses** the point.

If the ball ends **in court** on the **server's** side, the **server loses** the point.

If the ball ends **out of court** on the **server's** side, the **server wins** the point.
(i.e. as in tennis, but in this game the server makes all the moves!)

The player who first wins seven points wins the game provided she leads by a margin of two points.
If the score reaches six all, play continues until either player is two points ahead.
Players change ends (turn the book) after every six points.

illustrated by Viv Quillin   23

THE TRADESCANT TRUST

photographs by Norman Redfern

If you're at all interested in plants and gardening you may be familiar with Tradescantia, a trailing indoor plant. It was named after a seventeenth century gardener and botanist called John Tradescant, who brought it over from America.

His father, John Tradescant the elder, was gardener to Lord Salisbury in the seventeenth century and was sent to France to buy plants. He brought back oleanders, myrtles, figs, oranges and aubergines, and over 200 cypress trees. He also went to Holland bringing back roses, bulbs, mulberries and vines for the flower beds, orchards, fountains and terraces. Lord Salisbury died in 1612, and John Tradescant then worked in the garden of Sir Edward Wotton at St Augustine's Palace in Canterbury where, among the Canterbury Bells, he cultivated

melons, fennel from Italy, and a fine black cherry.

He was not only a gardener, but also a knowledgeable botanist, travelling to North Africa and to Russia on a diplomatic mission where he saw wild roses, the dianthus superbus, angelica, dwarf dogwood and bilberry. He introduced the larch tree, which provided England with timber, and bark for tanning and turpentine. In 1619 he went to Algeria with an expedition against the Barbary corsairs who were sailing up to Cornwall and looting and burning peaceful villages. But instead of returning with pirates' heads, John Tradescant returned with flowers: gladioli, valerian, hypericum, and also apricots, and the Cos lettuce, brought from the Greek island of Cos.

By 1625, John was head

gardener to George Villiers, Duke of Buckingham, a favourite of Charles I. John accompanied Buckingham to Paris where the Duke was standing proxy for the King in his marriage to Henrietta Maria, sister of Louis XIII. In 1627 Buckingham was assassinated and Tradescant was appointed Keeper of His Majesty's Gardens, Vines and Silkworms at Oatlands, the palace of Henrietta Maria, who was nicknamed 'the Rose and Lily Queen' because she united the Rose of England with the Lily of France. At Oatlands John created an elegant garden with an arched walk 100 yards long, and orchards with nearly 500 fruit trees.

Once John Tradescant was well established he bought a large house in Lambeth, not far from the Archbishop's palace, across the Thames from Westminster, renaming it The Ark. In the four acres around the house, he cultivated all the plants he had introduced to England, and exchanged seeds with other gardeners to famous houses.

His son, also called John, inherited his love of gardening and he too became a collector and traveller. He went to America to the thriving colony of Virginia, a beautiful fertile land, bringing back with him the phlox, the lupin, the Michaelmas Daisy, the acacia, the American walnut, the red maple, the deciduous cypress, the tulip tree, the plane, lilacs, and Virginia creeper. He also brought back the strange plant that was named after him – the Tradescantia.

This window donated by the Glaziers Company shows the routes travelled by the Tradescants.

These Guides from 9th North Lambeth found the tomb of Captain Bligh, of the Bounty, in the memorial garden.

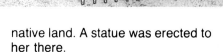

During their travels the Tradescants brought back other curiosities besides plants, and these were displayed in The Ark, which became the first public museum in London. Called the Museum of Rarities, it was one of the most popular places to visit in London. Charles I and his wife were among the first visitors and gave the museum many strange items from the royal wardrobes, including Henry VIII's cap, and Anne Boleyn's embroidered night cloak. After old John died his son carried on the work, adding extensively to the museum.

A powerful and ambitious neighbour of the Tradescants, Elias Ashmole, decided he wanted the museum himself, and he persuaded John to sign the museum over to him, in spite of objections by John's wife. Although John repudiated the deed of gift in his will, Ashmole harassed his widow, until she was forced to hand over the rarities. Ashmole then bequeathed the collection to Oxford as the foundation of the Ashmolean Museum, with no acknowledgement of the courage and energy put into the collection by the Tradescants. Only recently has this injustice been righted.

The Tradescants were buried in a tomb in the churchyard of St Mary-at-Lambeth. The church is mostly eighteenth century, but the tower was built in the fourteenth century, and the first church on the site was built in 1062 for the sister of Edward the Confessor.

During the past few decades St Mary's was badly neglected, and in 1972 it was closed and deconsecrated. It gradually fell into a state of dereliction, and a demolition order was passed for November 1976. The church was dirty, and the roof full of holes, the churchyard was overgrown and rubbish had been dumped there. The windows and porch were boarded up and the church was crumbling away.

However, early in 1976 Mrs. Rosemary Nicholson, who had always been interested in the Tradescant family, came on a pilgrimage to Lambeth, to visit the site of Tradescant's house and garden and see the tomb. Horrified by the state of the church and yard, Mrs. Nicholson decided to try and save the church and so founded the Tradescant Trust.

The Trust is now working to turn the church into a Museum of Gardening History, and the churchyard into the Tradescant Memorial Garden. Already a lot of hard work has raised sufficient funds for a new roof and the stonework has been cleaned up.

One of the aims of the Trust is to hold exhibitions in the church. The first was held in 1981, the 350th anniversary of the death of Captain John Smith, who had worked with the Tradescants and was captain of the ship that took John to Virginia. Captain Smith was captured by Red Indians, and would have been killed had not the Chief's young daughter, Pocahontas, pleaded with her father to spare his life, which he did. Pocahontas married John Rolfe, Captain Smith's lieutenant, and came back to England with him, where she was presented at court. But sadly she became ill in the cold, damp climate and died in Gravesend on her way back to her native land. A statue was erected to her there.

In the winter of 1980/81 the Trust received a gift towards the cost of the restoration of the garden, but it was specified that it should not be used for employing a landscape architect. This was a problem, but by happy coincidence the Queen Mother had visited the garden in 1977 accompanied by Lady Salisbury, who asked the Trust if she could help them. The Trust now decided to consult her about the design of the restored garden. After studying the churchyard, Lady Salisbury submitted to the Trust a plan for the area, which they happily accepted.

A team of volunteers, working under Lady Salisbury, started restoring the garden as a memorial to the Tradescants, putting in only plants that would have been available in the seventeenth century, and plants that the Tradescants discovered.

How strange that Lady Salisbury is making a garden round the tombs of the men who designed her ancestors' gardens long ago.

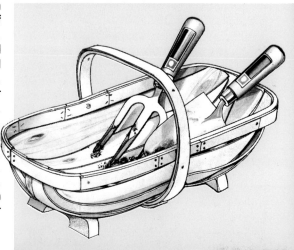

illustrations by Craig Warwick

Music with Crescendo Pink

continued from page 14

Clementine improved week by week in a most startling way, and by the end of October, just five months after she had first held a violin, she was playing Paganini's Violin Concerto No 1 in D, a very difficult piece of music.

Windows above and below her twentieth floor flat were flung wide open whenever she practised, neighbours clapped and cheered and soon she was the talk of the district. But Clementine did not believe she did it herself. She believed it came from the odd feverish tingling that came over her when she began to play. It was as though the bow took over and she followed it wherever it wanted to go. She tried to explain this to Miss Pink: "It's when I use my bit of rosin," she said. But Miss Pink refused to listen.

"My dear thing," replied Crescendo Pink, "I pride myself on being able to teach *anyone*. And with a Rarivarius, you cannot go wrong. You were made to play the violin, that's obvious!"

"I'd rather play the piano," said Clementine.

Crescendo Pink ignored the remark and drew a long sheet of paper from a drawer. "I've entered you for the Gifted Children's Orchestra Christmas Recital at the Albert Hall, on December the twenty-first. Get your father or mother to sign this form and bring it back to me. We'll get your picture in the evening paper a little later, and an interview on television, and we'll launch you on a musical career par excellence!" said Miss Pink, forecasting the years ahead.

"But it's not me, honestly. It's the rosin. I can't do it!" Clementine was alarmed at the very idea of being thought of as a gifted child.

"What trish-trash you talk," said Miss Pink, brushing the protests aside. "The rosin indeed! Now that's enough for this evening. I have to sort out the music for the concert, so you dash off home and do some extra practising, there's a good girl. And take the bus," she added, giving Clementine twenty pence. "It's raining. You mustn't get the violin wet."

Clementine took her at her word and dashed off so fast that she fell over on the pavement by the bus stop. In her confusion, she had to put up a leg to signal to the approaching bus, while she grabbed at the bow of the Rarivarius, which had slipped out of the hastily fastened case.

When she reached the flats, she remembered the lift was out of order. It had been for the last four days. She had over one hundred steps to climb, and when she came to her own door, it was locked. Her father sometimes worked late on Fridays, but her mother should have been in.

Clementine was so tired that she slithered down the wall, pressing backwards until she was sitting on the ground. She felt in her blazer pocket for the paper Miss Pink had given her. It wasn't there, nor on the ground as far as she could see. She knew she must have lost it on the way home.

"I've got to find it. I've got to!" she thought in horror. "There'll be an awful row if I don't." She clattered back down the stairs, looking on every step. There was the usual litter, sweet papers and crisp packets, but no application form for the Gifted Children's Orchestra.

She was about halfway down when she heard slow footsteps coming up and muttered words of annoyance. Clementine leaned over the railing. It was her mother, and in her hand she held a piece of paper.

"Mum, you've found it!" Clementine hurried down, her voice echoing loudly on the bleak staircase.

Her mother looked up, surprised. "You're home early," she said. "I just popped over to the library. Here, I found this in the lobby. It's got your name on it and it's for the Henry Hall."

"Albert," corrected Clementine.

"That's what I said."

When Clementine explained about the special concert for gifted children, her mother almost crowed with delight at her talented daughter, and rushed joyfully to tell Mr Hall the moment he came in from work.

But Clementine's troubles were not over. After dinner, when it was time to practise, she could not find the box of rosin. It was not in her violin case. Then she knew it must have rolled out when she had fallen over at the bus stop.

Clementine did not dare to play the violin without the special rosin and she spent the whole evening taking extra care with her homework instead.

The following morning, she set off for school earlier than usual, and ran first to the bus stop near Miss Pink's house. But the ivory box was not there. Certainly a beautiful little box like that would not have been overlooked by anybody passing by. Clementine searched the clogged gutter and the garden hedges nearby; but the rosin was nowhere to be found. It seemed to her like the end of the world.

For the rest of the week Clementine felt sick every morning when she woke. Her mother wondered why she had gone off her food and tried to coax her with all the latest breakfast cereals, like Nutty Chocolate Wheat, and Marshmallow Rice Pops, and Chewing-Gum Flavoured Oat Snaps. But Clementine pushed them all aside.

"You can't live without food, child. Nobody can," said her mother in exasperation, when she had run out of cereal ideas.

"I'll try," Clementine said, weakly. She thought it might be better to fade away before she had to face Crescendo Pink on Friday evening. It was hard enough trying to find excuses at home for not practising. She complained of muscle cramp in her arms, neckache, backache, earache, headache and chinache, until her mother decided she would take her daughter to the doctor first thing Saturday morning.

Clementine found no help at school either. A broken arm in P.E. would have come in very useful... but it didn't happen.

Thursday night was anguish for her. When the first morning light peeped in through her curtains, Clementine hid her head under the bedcovers to keep Friday away; but eight o'clock came round as it

26

always did and her mother called her. Slowly she climbed out of bed, took the Rarivarius and went into her clothes cupboard. Pulling the door over, so that she would not be heard, she softly tried out *Twinkle, Twinkle*. It sounded like nothing on earth – or in heaven. It was as though she had picked up the instrument for the very first time.

Somehow she got through the day at school doing everything in a dream. At quarter to six she dragged her feet along the pavement to the big grey house of Crescendo Pink. "I could run away," she thought. "Or maybe jump on the wrong bus and keep going." But she had nothing with her, no toothbrush, not even the money for a bus fare. She rang the bell and stood trembling, like an old engine ticking over.

She had a long wait and was about to turn away with relief, when the door opened. Crescendo Pink stood there, entirely wrapped in newspaper. She was recognisable only by her eyes, which were staring out through two holes cut in the paper. Her voice was a thick mumble behind the rustling paper as she waved Clementine away with one arm.

"No child! No! *Shoo! Shoo!* It's Friday the thirteenth. I explained to your mother. I *never*, positively *never* teach on Friday the thirteenth," she said.

Clementine forgot her troubles for a moment and tried not to laugh at the extraordinary sight. The draped newspapers were joined together with Sellotape and some were very old, in varying shades of yellow.

"Please, Miss Pink," she began, hiding a smile. "What's the paper for?" She thought of Jack with his head in vinegar and brown paper, but there was no smell of vinegar.

"It's the dates, dear thing. I'm covered with dates of eights. Got to obliterate today altogether. I'm done out in all the eights I could get hold of; my lucky number, d'you see? It's the only way to avert disaster. Even the air could be fatal for me today." She slammed the door and shouted out through the letterbox, "Come next week! Keep practising."

"What an odd sort of person," Clementine murmured. "Must be because she's brilliant, Mum said."

With this fortunate reprieve, she skipped all the way home, trying not to think that she would have to go through it all over again in a week's time. Her spirits had risen by the time she reached the flats. She found her father brighter than she had seen him in weeks, and her mother was rosy with excitement.

"Oh, I am glad," she was saying. "I never did feel happy up here, like a parrot's nest on a ship."

"Crow's," said Mr Hall. "Course not. People weren't meant to live in the clouds. I reckon that's what's wrong with our Clemmy. You'll see, she'll get her appetite back when we get down to earth again."

"What's all this, Mum? Dad?" asked Clementine, putting her violin case in the hall stand.

"Oh Clemmy, we're moving. Your Dad's been transferred to Axminster to work on a new kind of carpet, that's going to be washable, mothproof, dustproof, dogproof, catproof…"

"Hold it! Hold it! Alright, dear, isn't there something more to the point we have to tell Clementine?" said her father, shuffling his feet uncomfortably on the rug.

"Oh, my! Yes! We're ever so sorry, Clemmy, but you'll have to give up your lessons with Crescendo Pink. We'll be too far away. And we won't be here for the concert at the Henry Hall, unless you travel back specially."

"Albert. Crumbs! Isn't that awful! The very e-eend," groaned Clementine, pulling a face as long as her fiddle. "I'll never get over this! Still, it's better than the world coming to an end."

"The what? I knew you'd be disappointed, Clemmy, but don't fret. We'll make it up to you. Look, I've made your favourite fried bread soup, I've got an out-size chicken nearly ready in the oven, and afterwards, gooseberry pie with ice-cream."

"And if that's not enough," put in her father, "I think we should buy a piano. We'll have plenty of room for one in the new place."

"Wow-eeeee!" shouted Clementine. That evening she ate one of the biggest dinners of her life.

Crescendo Pink was sorry to lose her star pupil, but she brightened up like a star herself when Clementine, thankful she would never have any further use for it, presented her with the Rarivarius violin.

"I'm sorry about the rosin, though," Clementine said. "I lost it."

"Not to worry, dearest thing," said Miss Pink, stroking some of her own rosin on the bow. "I don't need the rosin."

Clementine whispered softly to herself, "No, you don't, but I did."

Crescendo Pink was well away into Groch Capusta's *Air for a Rare Violin* in E flat, with her ringlets jumping about like springs, and her head darting about as if it might come off. Her eyes were tightly shut and she was smiling euphorically. She reminded Clementine of herself during those few magical weeks when she had tingled with violin energy.

Slowly, she stepped backwards out of the room, blowing a goodbye kiss to the unseeing eyes of Crescendo Pink. She silently closed the front door of the big grey house and walked away towards the warm glow in the western sky.

illustrated by Viv Quillin

Most Guides (and Guiders!) who go camping hope to avoid two things in particular – rain and insects!

Rain, rain, go away!

If you look closely at the fabric of your tent you will see lots of little holes – so how does it keep out the the rain?

A nylon tent keeps out the rain because it is lined with a waterproof material such as polyurethane. The trouble with this is that as well as preventing rain coming into the tent, it also stops water vapour inside the tent getting out. Instead, the vapour condenses on the inside of the tent, making it damp. For this reason, nylon tents are not usually used by Guide Companies. Canvas tents are much more suitable for living in.

A canvas tent allows moisture inside the tent to pass out through all the little holes in the weave. When it rains, the threads of the canvas swell slightly as they absorb water, and as they swell the tiny gaps close up until the holes are too small to allow any water through. In this way the canvas forms a waterproof barrier. Most older tents use this method to keep the rain out and are quite reliable unless you touch the side of the tent when it is raining. Then water will start coming through and the tent will leak until it has had a chance to dry out. Once it is dry it will be properly waterproof next time it rains.

Canvas can also be waterproofed by coating the threads with a waxy substance which fills up much of the holes between them, but still leaves enough of a gap for the water vapour to escape. Because the proofing material is waxy, water does not soak into it, but remains as droplets on the surface and runs off.

Keeping dry

When you get up in the morning at camp the grass will almost certainly be wet. This is caused by dew which occurs on clear, still nights. When the sun sets, the earth cools rapidly, especially if there is not much cloud to keep in the warmth. As the layer of air nearest to the earth cools, some of the water vapour in the air condenses onto the ground, forming drops of dew. If the temperature falls below 0°C the dew will freeze and the ground will have a layer of frost. (Not while you're camping, I hope!)

Keep your feet dry in the early dewy morning by wearing Wellingtons, or plimsolls without socks. As your feet are waterproof, it is easier to dry them off than a pair of soggy socks.

When it rains, just for fun make yourself a waterproof hat out of tin foil – any shape you like!

Plastic bags

If your rucksack is old it may not be fully waterproof, so line it with a large plastic bag (a bin liner?), and put everything into that. If you keep different items such as socks inside separate plastic bags inside the main bag, it makes things much easier to find.

A plastic bag can also be used as a washing-up bowl, using rocks to support the edges. Fill the centre with warm water to rinse your cup and plates.

A cracked or broken egg can be put in a plastic bag and cooked in boiling water.

Guaranteed waterproof

Waterproof cloth was invented in 1823 by a Scot called Charles Macintosh. He found a way of using naphtha and rubber together to make cloth which water did not penetrate. Previous attempts at making a rubberised cloth had failed since, as well as being sticky and smelly, the cloth melted if the wearer stood near a fire – most unsuitable for camp!

Wellingtons

Another waterproof item essential for the comfort of many campers is the Wellington boot. The original Wellingtons were riding boots worn by the Duke of Wellington (1769–1852), but now the name refers to any loose-fitting, calf-high rubber boot.

Paper

It may seem surprising to you, but newspaper can be a useful item to have around when there's water about. As well as being rolled into 'logs' and used as kindling to get a fire going, it can also be woven into a sitter to keep you dry when you sit on the ground, and if it is scrunched up and stuffed into the toes of damp boots and shoes it helps to dry them out more quickly.

Paper bags are useful at camp, too. Did you know it is possible to boil water, and even cook in a paper bag? If liquid is heated over a fire in a paper bag or paper cup (not the waxed sort), the bag will not burn where the liquid touches it. If the fire touches any other part of the bag, it will burn, so keep the upper part of the bag away from any flames.

Cook your breakfast in a paper bag

Line the bottom of the bag with two or three strips of bacon. Break an egg into the bag over the bacon. Fold down the top of the bag and push a thin stick through the fold. Hold the bag over the embers of your fire by the stick. Don't try to cook like this over a flaming fire as this will result in a very burnt breakfast! Get a good bed of embers going before you begin and watch out for any sudden flaring. When your breakfast is cooked, you can try boiling water for tea or coffee (in another bag of course!). Be careful that the top of the bag doesn't scorch; keep the bag a reasonable distance from the fire all the time.

CREEPING CREATURES

If you have any sense, you won't pitch your tent over an anthill, or on a molehill, but no matter how carefully you choose a quiet, uninhabited-looking part of a field, there will be creatures lurking under your tent! Scientists have estimated that in just one acre of English farmland there could be between 7 and 8 million insects! Altogether on Earth there are about one million insects to every human being!

Over 20,000 different species of insects have been identified in the UK; the following are some of the ones you might meet at camp.

Ants, like campers, live in highly organised groups! Most British ants are vegetarian and unable to sting, so should not worry you too much. But in Africa, Soldier Ants march through the countryside looking for prey, and will attack anything that gets in their way, eating birds, lizards, snakes and grasshoppers. Our ants are more likely to eat bread and sugar, so be sure to keep food in ant-proof

containers, and try not to leave crumbs.

Slugs are usually thought of with distaste, but they're not all bad! Some slugs eat decaying plants, rotten wood, and even fungi, and others eat grubs that feed on healthy flowers and vegetables. Of course, some slugs are a pest too; they are the ones with a taste for strawberries!

Wasps love jam and marmalade so always wipe jars clean before putting them away in the store tent. Keep any opened packets of such items as sugar in a tin or similar airtight container.

The other point to remember when dealing with wasps is *Don't Panic!* If you are unlucky enough to be stung, remove the sting if it is still in, then apply an antihistamine cream such as Wasp-Eze, or bathe the area with a solution of bicarbonate of soda.

Bee stings can be soothed with lemon juice or honey. If you can see the sting, scrape it out with a fingernail, or remove it with tweezers. Don't try to press it out as this will just push the poison further in. Very occasionally people are allergic to bee stings, and if this is the case medical help should be sought.

Worms are essential for the well-being of the soil, keeping it ventilated and drawing decaying vegetation down into it. There will be thousands of worms in your camping field all busily at work. According to a well known song, worms are believed to be highly nutritious!

Flies can be very troublesome at camp, as their feeding habits make them dangerous carriers of disease. They particularly enjoy investigating decaying food, so be sure to deal with any waste immediately. They also have a nasty habit of laying their eggs on fresh meat, so if you do have to store any for a short time (and it's always best to cook fresh meat at once), ensure it is well protected by making a fly-proof larder using muslin. Make use of tin foil and cling film too, when storing foodstuffs.

Millipedes The name 'millipede' means 'thousand feet', which is rather an overstatement since none of them has more than 200. Some of the earliest millipedes on Earth were two metres long, but the largest surviving ones are only about 30 cms and fortunately are found only in the Seychelles, not on English campsites!

Centipedes Unlike the millipede, which is a vegetarian and eats the roots of young plants, centipedes are regarded as friends by gardeners, if not by Guides, because they eat grubs and other plant-destroying insects. Centipedes are flatter than millipedes and have only one pair of legs to each segment of their body; millipedes have two pairs.

Earwigs are nocturnal, but as they often choose to hide in obvious places during the day, they're frequently disturbed by disconcerted Guides. A favourite place is a cosy fold of canvas in a brailed tent. However, they quickly run away, as they are known to have an aversion to high-pitched screams!

Spiders really deserve to be better liked as they are extremely active insect destroyers. Nearly every creature they eat means the end of a pest. So you should pay heed to the traditional saying: 'If you wish to live and thrive, let the spider run alive', because that spider may be about to catch that pesky fly!

HAPPY CAMPING!

National Youth Theatre of Great Britain

by Cecilia Fellner

photographs by Nobby Clark

The National Youth Theatre's letterheading would assure anyone of its respectability in the world of visual and performing arts:

Patron The Earl of Snowdon,
President Sir Ralph Richardson.

But it is Michael Croft's dedication as Founder / Director which has produced the consistently high standard of production no other spontaneous group of young people could hope to achieve. If you cannot join the NYT do try and see at least one of the performances each year. It could be that you know the work already as most of the plays are chosen specially to coincide with school and examination syllabuses.

Here are some scenes from 1982 productions. *The Crucible* (Arthur Miller) was performed at the Jeannetta Cochrane Theatre; *Murder in the Cathedral* (T. S. Eliot) in St Pancras Parish Church; *Macbeth* and *The Bread and Butter Trade* (Peter Terson, author of *Zigger Zagger*) at the Shaw Theatre.

In addition to seven main productions, members aged 17–20 gave three studio productions, and presentations were made by the intermediate group, aged 15–16, and the junior group, 14–15. No one gets to play a big role in their first year, whatever their

age, but they can gain valuable experience in these off-stage productions. For instance, an audience of 250 watched the Intermediate Course's final presentation in a gym one very warm summer afternoon. They improvised on the theme of Buskers. This provided a strong storyline with conflict situations involving the council, the press and local cops (no, not real policemen!) and offered plenty of scope for great singing, dancing and mime. The only costumes used were caps and bowler hats. The effect was quite fantastic.

31

The Bread and Butter Trade

Murder in the Cathedral

Macbeth

You could find yourself travelling abroad with NYTGB. Since 1960 the Company has been on tour each year to at least one of the following countries: Holland, France, Italy, Germany, Denmark, Canada and the United States of America!

I took these colour photographs in the gym at Haverstock Hill School, the NYT's main rehearsal centre, last August. Michael Croft is seen welcoming 600 young people at the start of their London season, introducing the producers and the sponsors, Texaco, and explaining what he hopes might be achieved.

You will have seen some of the actors who made their first public appearance with this Company – Martin Jarvis, Helen Mirren, Diana Quick, Barry Rutter, Simon Ward, to name a few – but such a degree of personal success is extremely rare and not in fact the main purpose of the NYT. It is far more important and rewarding to work together as a team, make new friendships, gain practical theatrical experience in your own field and become useful members of the Company.

You could find you had been selected from thousands of applicants in spite of a very shaky audition, because you seemed to have the essential vitality, individuality and endurance, so there is no need to despair because you haven't developed a beautiful speaking voice or a smashing figure.

Michael Croft does ask members to be punctual and reliable, leave any anti-social attitudes behind, and generally behave well enough to avoid getting thrown out of digs or becoming exhausted from attending parties late in the evening. As you can see, there's no need to go outside this cheerful, informal group to have a great time, even if it means working a seven-day week in the holidays.

Unfortunately most plays have more acting roles for boys, but more girls apply, so you could find yourself working on costumes, scenery or lighting instead, but this does provide valuable training for stage designers and technicians – many former NYT members now work in television.

Membership is open to anyone between 14 and 20 years of age, and selection is by interview and audition: no academic qualifications are necessary. Interview centres are in London, Bristol, Manchester, Birmingham, Belfast, Swansea, Newcastle, Aberdeen and Edinburgh. Someone at school will know where to send your applications which must arrive by the end of January in any year.

ACTIVITIES AT GLENBROOK

Glenbrook House was bought by the Girl Guides Association in 1967 to provide a centre for training in outdoor activities. Situated in the Derbyshire Peak National Park, near Hathersage, the grounds cover nine acres accommodating six camp sites.

I visited Glenbrook during Guide Week, when Guides are allowed to try activities that are normally only for Rangers.

Canoeing photos by Joan Randall

The first archery lesson.

Archery

To begin with, I watched a group of Guides from Worcestershire having their first archery lesson. They were pretty hopeless at first, but quickly improved. By the time they let fly their twelfth arrow, most of them were hitting the target, and at the end of the lesson everyone had hit it at least once.

I asked the Guides how they were enjoying their stay at Glenbrook. ''Great!'' was the unanimous verdict. During their week's stay they intended to try every activity. The previous day they'd been canoeing, and after the archery some of them were going rock climbing. The younger ones were going down to Bamford to watch the sheepdog trials. Later in the week there would be pot-holing, pony trekking and hill walking. I wondered whether they'd have the energy left to strike camp!

Betty Carradus, Guider in charge at Glenbrook, teaches archery. The target seems a long way away!

photographs by Nigel Robertson

Kate and Susan have a breather before their second climb.

Left: Steve explains to Kate how to wear the abseiling ropes.

Concentrating hard, Kate starts to abseil.

Nichole negotiates a difficult section of the rock face.

During lunch hour the 1st Beighton Guides arrived. They had stayed at Glenbrook before and were excitedly discussing the new activities they wanted to try. Some of them had been too young to go rock climbing last time — you have to be over fourteen for this.

Rock Climbing

The climbing takes place on a rocky outcrop up on the moor. When I arrived the Guides were putting on the necessary protective helmets. They offered to lend me some climbing shoes and a hard hat, but I decided I'd rather watch from ground level!

Before they began, the instructor, Steve, explained a little about the techniques of climbing. He said they should use their legs and feet to push up, rather than pulling themselves with their arms. Also they should try not to cling to the rock face as this would tend to push their feet outwards. By leaning slightly away from the rock they would find it much easier to keep their feet in the cracks. The final instruction was to look for the easiest handholds. This seemed obvious to the Guides, but Steve explained that once up on the rock face it was not difficult to miss the best handholds.

He stressed how important it was to have proper instruction before attempting any climbing. It could be very dangerous for someone who didn't know what they were doing or had not brought the right gear.

Steve then made the first climb. It looked easy the way he went up, the Guides attentively watching where he put his hands and feet, but when their turn came they all found it quite difficult. Each Guide was roped as she went up, just in case, but no one slipped.

Steve told them to jam their feet into cracks to get a good foothold, and not to rest on their knees. He explained that if they climbed onto a narrow ledge on their knees, they would be unable to push up from that position. By putting their feet on the ledge, they could then straighten their legs and go higher.

The Guides made two more moderate climbs up different parts of the cliff face, and then tried abseiling. It was certainly much quicker coming down!

37

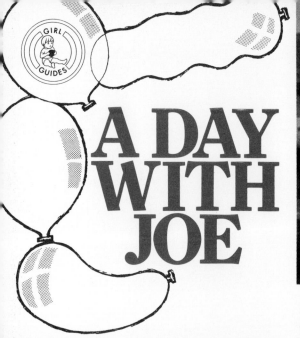

A DAY WITH JOE

If you are considering taking the Child Care badge you will know that it requires you to plan a day for a three to five year old, recognising the importance of regular routine, and that you must take charge of a child or small group of children for part of a day. These slides show a typical day in the life of toddler Joe. Joe was born on December 24th 1979 and lives with his Mum, Diana, and his Dad, John, in Surrey.

photographs by Norman Redfern

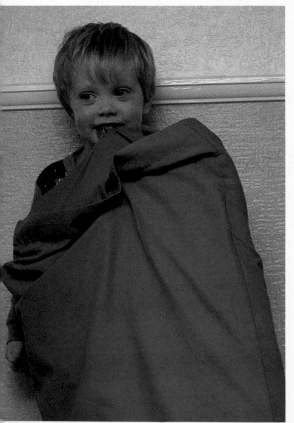

1 Joe wakes up early, bursting with energy. He sleeps in the lower of two bunk beds, but once he's awake he likes to climb onto the top bunk with some of his toys (or his blue pillow!) until it's time to get up. Joe gets washed and dressed with a little help from Diana. Young children are often very slow at dressing themselves, but it's best not to help unless really necessary as they must learn how to do up buttons and tie laces. Clothes should be warm but light, and allow freedom of movement. It's also important that they are washable!

2 In the kitchen Joe enjoys helping Diana with the washing-up. He takes extra care washing his own dish. The kitchen can be a dangerous place for young children so they should never be left unsupervised. Care should always be taken to ensure that sharp knives, bottles of bleach and other dangerous items are either locked away, or well out of reach (and don't forget toddlers like to climb!).

3,4 Usually Joe plays outside for part of the day, but as it was too wet to go in the garden, he stayed inside with his space mobile. The space mobile is quite a sophisticated toy, but Joe also likes to play with his bricks, soft toy animals, cardboard boxes, toy cars, and a simple wooden train set. It's not always the most exciting toy that brings the most joy – sometimes it's not even a toy at all. Joe loves to play with a crocodile oven glove!

5   In the afternoon, Diana and Joe go shopping in the supermarket. Joe likes to ride in the trolley, and looks forward to the trip as he is allowed to choose something good to eat. Young children should be encouraged to eat fresh fruit and vegetables. Joe like apples and celery, and on this occasion he wants a red pepper.

6   Milk is also a valuable part of a child's diet and as Joe doesn't like it very much, Diana makes him banana milkshakes. Joe's particularly fond of bananas and chooses the biggest bunch he can find.

7   Back home again, Diana makes an apple pie and Joe has a piece of pastry to play with. Small children find it easier to play on the floor than on a table top, so Joe has a special board.

8   After tea, Joe crayons for a little while. It's important that children don't get too excited before bed, or they may not be able to sleep. A quiet activity such as colouring or doing a jigsaw is best at this time.

9   Bathtime over, Joe gets into his pyjamas and chooses a storybook.

10   Joe takes the book downstairs to ask his Dad to read to him. John tucks him into bed and reads to him until he falls asleep.

Top: Bullet train, so-called on account of its shape and high speed, and temple in Kyoto. Photographs courtesy of Japan National Tourist Organisation

Left: Hie shrine and uniform of the Girl Scouts of Japan, illustrated by Kathleen Whapham

Below: Hiroko Ito, a Girl Scout from Kumamoto Troop 3, visited London for Folk Fest 10 and performed a beautiful traditional dance called Fu Musumi, Lady of the Wisteria (phot by Mary Vaughan) and schoolgirls with cherry blossom

JAPAN, LAND OF THE RISING SUN

by Shireen Bonner

Japan is a country of great contrasts, blending as it does ancient cultures and traditions which are still upheld and respected, with some of the most advanced technology in the world. Mention of the country can conjure up visions of delicate tea ceremonies and ancient martial arts as well as computerised machinery and fast cars.

Japan is made up of a chain of islands in the shape of a crescent which lie in the North Pacific close to the eastern fringe of the Asian continent. The four major islands, which are surrounded by about 3,000 smaller ones, are Honshu, Shikoko, Kyushu and Hokkaido. The landscape is very varied, with beautiful coastlines, volcanic mountains and deep, fertile valleys. Mount Fuji is probably the most famous natural wonder in Japan, along with the five lakes at its northern base.

Although Japan enjoys a temperate climate, the seasons are very distinct. There is a long rainy season, and in winter there are heavy snows and typhoons, which are a particular hazard to rice farmers. Spring is the best time of year to visit Japan, when the famous cherry blossoms are in flower. It is also the season for traditional festivities associated with flowers. The Girls' Festival is held annually on March 3rd and the Boys' is celebrated on May 5th. Cherry dances are presented at this time of year in Kyoto, the ancient capital of Japan.

Japanese traditions are everywhere in evidence, even in the highly-developed metropolis of Tokyo, the present-day capital. Tokyo boasts elaborate landscaped and miniature gardens, as well as ancient traditional theatres. Young people are encouraged to take an interest in the traditions as well as enjoying more modern activities. Sport and outdoor exercise play an important part in Japanese life. As well as the more familiar sports such as table tennis and badminton, Judo, Kendo, Karate, Sumo and Aikido are practised, by both boys and girls. These martial arts, which have their origins in self defence, can be very dangerous if not taught properly.

In Japan it is thought important to encourage group activities among young people, and groups and organisations are given financial assistance and special facilities. The Girl Scouts of Japan go back a long way. The Guide Movement started there in 1919, and in 1920 the Association took the name Nippon Joshi Hodadan, meaning Girl Guides of Japan. Nippon (or Nihon) is the name the Japanese use for their country and it has a lovely meaning – 'place from where the sun rises'. Their Guide Movement started in Tokyo, but soon spread throughout the country, and Japan became a founder member of the World Association of Girl Guides and Girl Scouts in 1928. The Movement was banned in the 1930s and early 40s, but in 1947 it was restarted by some former Guides. Troops were formed all over the country and the Girl Scouts of Japan were established in 1949.

Every summer, camp sessions and training courses are held at the national camp centre in the Togakushi Highlands, and international visitors often have the opportunity to camp there in beautiful surroundings. An important part of the Guiding programme in Japan is knowledge of the workings of the United Nations and the Girl Scouts of Japan co-operate with UNICEF and UNESCO.

Flower arranging, known as Ikebana or Kado, and the famous Tea Ceremony, the Chanoyu, are still popular among young women and girls in Japan. These two arts have mystical origins, and are not simply meaningless ceremonies designed for effect, although of course they can be learnt for this reason. They are meant to promote serenity and tranquility and are still practised seriously by young women as part of the social graces needed for marriage!

It is not necessary to be familiar with traditional Japanese etiquette to fit into society there, but Japan is a land of protocol based on simple courtesy. Handshakes and hugs are not commonly exchanged in public, and it is considered polite at least to offer to remove your shoes before entering someone else's house. It is considered impolite to look into the kitchen in the home you are visiting!

Japanese cuisine is considered to be among the best in the world. Food is always presented delicately and with great skill, so it not only tastes delicious, it looks wonderful – sometimes too good to eat! Japanese food should never be hurried, but savoured to the last mouthful. In a restaurant it is usual to have your food prepared at the table in front of you. This could be tender, marinated meat or fish, chopped into slivers at lightning speed, then very lightly fried by a skilled chef while you sit back and sip *sake* – Japanese rice wine. Fish is very common, and – yes – it can be eaten raw! However, it does need some preparation and should not be tried at home! Chopsticks are used to eat this traditional food. Of course, if you prefer a hamburger and chips instead, you will find them quite easily. Japanese towns and cities cater for practically all tastes in food.

It would be true to say that Japan is like nowhere else on earth. Elegance and grace are natural characteristics, and the courtesy and serenity of the Japanese people and their way of life has its roots firmly in the past, while adapting itself perfectly to the modern world.

Dear Captain,

by Angie Griffiths

---

29 Smelting la
Tinbridge Nor

July 2nd

Dear Captain,

You probably won't remember me. (I left the 7th Greenvale Company nearly a year ago). But this is to let you know some very good news. I am coming back! My family is moving back in the middle of August. This means I shall be able to re-join the Guides and meet all my old friends again. I bet Daffodil Patrol has been half-dead without me. And I expect you have missed me like mad. But you won't admit it.

Yours truly
Winifred Huggins

P.S. It must be nearly time for Guide camp. I wonder whether there are any spare places?

Honeysuckle House,
Park Road. Greenvale.

July 6th

Dear Winifred,

I certainly do remember you! You are imprinted on my mind forever! What a shock to hear you are moving back to liven up our little town of Greenvale. This is something I felt sure would never happen. I cannot find words to describe how I feel. My brain is quite numb.

It may surprise you to know that Daffodil Patrol has managed very well while you have been away. Better than ever before, in fact. And (you are quite right) even if I _had_ missed you like mad I would never admit it.

Yours sincerely,

Captain
Captain.

P.S. Yes it is nearly time for Guide camp. It is completely booked up, I'm glad to say.

---

29 Smelting la
Tinbridge Nor

July 10th

Dear Captain,

I have just heard. Samantha Thicket-Wicket has got chicken pox! Poor spotty Samantha. lucky me! Now I shall be able to come to camp. By the time you get this you will have had my mother's letter. She very keen for me to go to camp. All my family are k for me to go. Dad says it's pity camp doesn't last for six months or more. They'll miss me like mad, when the time comes. But they will ne admit it.

I expect it made your day, knowing I could come to cam I'll be ever such a helper. Y be amazed. yours truly Winifred

P.S. How's your foot?

Honeysuckle House.
Park Road. Greenvale.

July 14th

Dear Winifred,

Thank you for your letter.
Further to your mother's letter to me and my phone call to her, I can now confirm that you have a place at Guide camp. We are going to Cornwall again this year, from August 23rd to 30th.

But I must warn you - I want no trouble this year. We will have no rude songs round the camp-fire, and no crude jokes over breakfast. I am still getting letters from angry parents about what happened last year. This time I shall not put you in charge of loading the tent poles in to the coach. I can still remember that feeling of horror a year ago when we had just arrived in the far reaches of Cornwall and you told me that the tent poles were still back on the pavement in Greenvale. It was pitch dark and teeming with rain. And your hysterics only made things worse.
Perhaps this year we can all remain calm when things go wrong. (And they're bound to, now!)

Yours sincerely,
Captain
Captain.

P.S. My foot is almost back to normal.
Please do not blame yourself for what happened with the mallet last year. My silly foot was too close to the tent-peg.

---

29 smelting lane
Tinbridge North
July 18th

Dear Captain,
Just a line to let you know sive started packing my gear for camp. I have put in my high-heeled silver sandals ready for the Disco on the last night. And sive bought a new nightie - it's pink lace with frills - and fluffy slippers to match. Mum reckons I won't be warm enough, but I know best.
Can I be in charge of collecting firewood again this year? And can I try out a few new recipes? I have packed some red peppers and fish in tin-foil especially.
Yours hopefully,
Winnie

P5 How are your knees?

Honeysuckle House.
Park Road. Greenvale.

July 22nd

Dear Winifred,

When packing for camp it might be a good idea to take the things written on your kit list. High-heeled sandals are not quite the thing for a muddy field, especially when we have to share the field with cows. You know what I mean!

I am sorry, but I shall not be able to let you loose to collect wood this year. The sound of you shouting 'Timber', and the sight of that huge beech tree crashing down last year was just too much to bear.

The cooking-list is already organised, I'm afraid. So we shall have to miss your fish-in-foil creation. Your toad-in-the-hole last year was a dish to be remembered! Real toad. How original. But it's the sort of treat one only needs once in a lifetime. You may, of course, help with the washing-up this year.

All good wishes,
Captain
Captain.

P.S. My knees are much better thank you.
Please do not feel awful about what happened last year when you served the food. The doctor says that the scar in the shape of a red-hot tin plate will soon fade.

---

29 Smelting lane
Tinbridge North.
July 26th

Dear Captain,

Thanks for your letters. Do you realise, it's only three more weeks until I arrive back in Greenvale. And soon after that it will be time for camp. I can hardly wait! I am busy practising my knots. Shanksheeps, hitched cloves and double-underhand. You never know --- you might want me to make a rope bridge over a ravine or something.
Will there be an all-night trek again this year? And may we have lots of games and competitions? Please say yes.
Yours excitedly,
Winnie

P.S. I'm getting quite good at First Aid. So if you have an accident at camp do come and find me.

Honeysuckle House.
Park Road. Greenvale.

July 30th

Dear Winifred,

   Yes, I do realise how soon we shall have the
pleasure of your company. I find it hard to
think of much else!

   I am determined that this year's camp will
be a success, so please, Winifred, try to abide
by the few rules we have. This time do <u>not</u>
leave the farm gates open. Those cows did a
dreadful lot of damage when they ran straight
through the village shop, and I am still having
nightmares about the court case which came up
last month. Also, do <u>not</u> try to carry a tray full
of eggs on your head again..... not while riding
a bike, anyway. And do <u>not</u> use your billy-can as
a helmet even if it is raining, I don't think the
hospital would be as sympathetic this time.

   You will be glad to hear there are plenty of
competitions and games planned. But please, this
year do not get so over-excited. It was such a
pity that my new boots were used in that Welly-
throwing competition. They were never quite the
same after I fished them out of that smelly pond.

   I'm not sure whether there will be an all-night
trek this year. I may have to go on my own all-
night trek..... just to get some peace.

                    Yours, Captain.

P.S. If I have an accident at camp I shall not
      need to come and find you. You are sure
      to be there already!

---

29 smelting
Tinbridge Nor
August 3rd

Dear Captain,
   Great! lots of fun and games
in store. Just what s need after
the dull time s've had here lately
I get so bored. People just don't
seem to appreciate me.
   s've got loads of energy that's
waiting to burst out at camp.
I'm like a spring that has been
held down. You'll see, s've got
some really lively plans for our camp
this time. It will be a week you
will never forget. you'll be glad
s came!

              Yours ever
                   Win

P.S. Remember when s let that bull
out last year. Mum says you should
<u>have</u> awarded yourself the Agility badge.
Isn't she a scream.?

Honeysuckle House.
Park Road. Greenvale.

August 7th

Dear Winifred,

   I beg you - no practical jokes this year,
please! It wasn't a bit funny last year when you
hid my torch and put slugs in my sleeping bag.
And I did not find it at all amusing when that
goat walked past, wearing my hair-net. As for the
cold porridge in my soap-bag.... the less said the
better. Nobody is wide-awake and at their best at
five in the morning, so it was quite unfair of you
to do what you did. I <u>know</u> everyone fell about
laughing. I <u>know</u> Samantha Thicket-Wicket split her
pyjamas, giggling. I <u>know</u> Peggy Kettle laughed
until she was sick. But it was NOT funny! Not at
the time, anyway.

              See you next week, no doubt.

                    Captain
                    Captain.

P.S. I think it would be best if you left your
      radio at home this year. We do not want
      trouble with stampeding sheep again.

---

29 smelting la
Tinbridge Nort
August 10t

Captain dear,
   Don't worry! I have unpacked my
radio and put my roller skates in.
instead. Skates will be much
quieter.
   Mum says she phoned you last
night for a chat and you told her
you'd been to the doctor. Why do
you feel all of a quiver? why've
you got a twitch? (what a funny
place no have a twitch.) why can
you get to sleep at night? Is there
a problem in your life — something
you just can't face? Perhaps s can
help. A Guide should always be a
helper.
   Only two more days, then you'll
see me standing on your doorstep.
That thought <u>MUST</u> cheer you up!
          See you soon
              Love, Win
P.S. I'm bringing Harry my pet
mouse to camp with me. Hope that's
okay. He is no trouble. Ever so
friendly. Eats anything, sleeps anyw
                    Win

Traditional COUNTRY CRAFTS

by Bernard Schofield

To us, country crafts mean either hobbies which have a traditional link with the countryside, like smocking, or those which involve using natural materials, such as basketry or rushwork.

To many country people, however, especially to those born in the early years of this century, country crafts were an integral part of the rural scene, in which the thatcher, saddler, hurdle-maker, broom-maker, hedge-layer, dry-stone wall builder and other country workers played an important role in the country economy. Such skills were not learnt from books, as crafts so often are today, but were handed down from parents to their children in an on-going process that altered little from one generation to the next.

Perhaps the most sought after country worker today is the thatcher, whose skills are much in demand in those parts of Britain where thatch can be found. These professionals are guaranteed plenty of work in repairing and renewing thatched roofs.

Methods of thatching have varied little over the years. Usually working in pairs, the thatchers begin at the eaves of the roof, one thatcher handing bundles of Norfolk reed or straw, called yealms, to the other up the ladder.

Another fascinating craft still in existence is that of making birch brooms or besoms. Sprays of birch twigs are first put aside to toughen and dry out over a period of months. The sprays are then broken to the required length and laid out in bundles. Binding the sprays to the handles is done using bonds made of hazel or withy which has been split and shaved into thick ribbons, and then soaked in water to render it pliable.

In certain parts of rural Britain, particularly in the northern counties of England and in Scotland and Wales, fields are enclosed by dry-stone walls. This type of wall is highly practical in

hilly and mountainous areas, where there is an abundance of out-lying stone and a lack of natural vegetation for hedgerows. A finely constructed dry-stone wall is an object of real beauty and requires considerable skill to make it an effective enclosure for animals.

The foundation of the wall is generally laid with two courses of the biggest stones which are of a fairly uniform size and shape. Then, building much as one would a brick wall, but using layers of stones of a lesser size as the wall grows higher, the courses are made to slope slightly inwards. The skill comes in fitting together stones of the right size, especially at the top of the wall where it is at its weakest. Building a dry-stone wall is slow and back-breaking work.

Finally, no review of traditional country crafts would be complete without mentioning the making of walking sticks, umbrella handles and other ornamental woodcraft; in days gone by this would have included shepherd's crooks.

Ash and oak are familiar woods often used in woodcraft, but for walking sticks chestnut is generally used. The process of turning a chestnut pole into a walking stick is a long one and begins with the seasoning of the wood. To form the handle, one end of the pole is heated in hot sand and pressed round an iron ring and left to set. The long part of the stick often needs straightening and this is also done by placing it in hot sand, for a day, and then in notches on a special 'horse' of wood. Once shaped, various treatments follow: including nosing, tapering, scouring with sand and water, bleaching and mottling. The finishing processes include the formation of dark and light rings round the stick, decorative carving, inlaid work, and finally dyeing and polishing.

There are many other traditional country crafts. Here are details of two which you can try for yourself.

Smocking

The white smock-frock of the farm labourer was once a common sight in the countryside. As a loose-fitting yoked garment, generally made from coarse linen, it was worn over or instead of a coat for protection while working in the fields. Smock-frocks were characteristically decorated with traditional ornamental patterns which were stitched over the gathers on the neck and sleeves. These patterns varied according to the county in which the smock was made. Nowadays the craft of smocking is mainly used to decorate children's clothes.

Preparing the gathers

The material is gathered up to form small regular pleats by drawing rows of running stitches through the material in straight lines (fig 1). It is best to buy a smocking transfer to give you a stitch guide. This is a piece of paper with rows of regularly spaced dots marked on it, which you iron on to the material. Using one line of thread for each line of dots, you pick up the dots with the needle until all have been threaded. You then draw up the various threads to produce the gathers. Wind the ends of the threads round pins to secure them temporarily.

Smocking designs

There are many stitches you can use in smocking. If you don't want to try any of the traditional patterns shown here, try inventing your own. Most embroidery stitches can be adapted for smocking. Try to make your design a mixture of straight and diagonal stitches, and use different colours of thread to make it really pretty. You can work out the design on paper first to guide you if you are unsure whether it will work.

Threads

The most suitable threads to use are those of stranded cotton, which you can use in varying thicknesses according to the weight of the material. With heavy linen, for example, it is best to use four strands. Three strands are best for cotton, and for fine material such as organdie, use two strands.

Stitches

The illustrations show a number of decorative stitches traditionally used in smocking. When you have finished the decorative stitches, draw out the gathering threads, and gently wash the material to remove the dots. When you have smocked a piece of material, you can incorporate it into a garment by using the smocked section as part of a pattern.

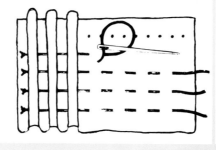

Gathering the pleats

Vandyke stitch

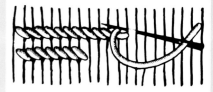

Outline stitch

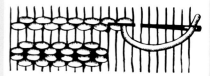

Cable and Double Cable stitch

Feather stitch

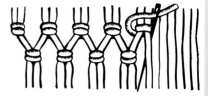

Honeycomb stitch

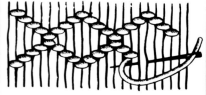

Wave and Trellis stitch

Diamond stitch

Corn Dollies

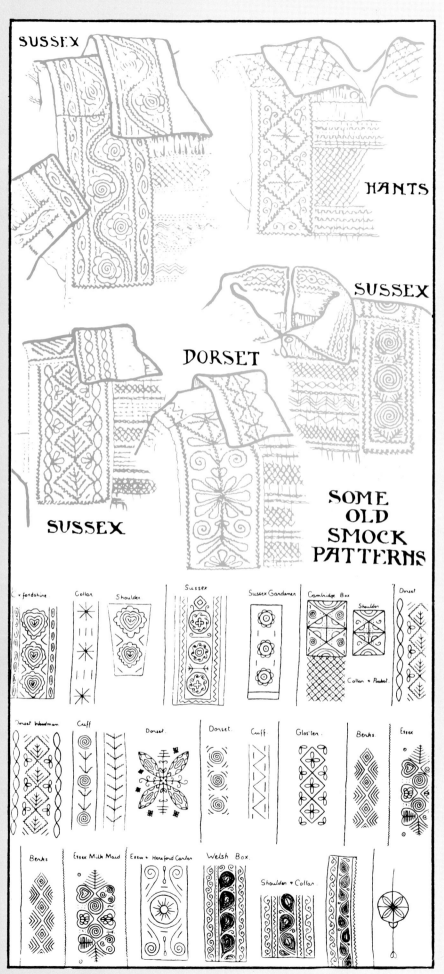

SUSSEX

HANTS

SUSSEX

DORSET

SUSSEX

SOME OLD SMOCK PATTERNS

Oxfordshire · Collar · Shoulder · Sussex · Sussex Gardener · Cambridge Box · Shoulder · Dorset

Dorset Woodman · Cuff · Dorset · Dorset · Cuff · Glos'ter · Berks · Essex

Collar + Pocket

Berks · Essex Milk Maid · Essex + Hereford Carter · Welsh Box · Shoulder + Collar

Corn dollies in one form or another have been made by people all over the world for thousands of years. Wherever cereal crops were grown it was customary for farmers to give part of the harvest – the first fruits – to God, as an offering of thanks when all had been safely gathered in. Traditionally the corn cut from the last sheaf at harvest time was plaited into symbolic figures representative of the various religious beliefs. Corn dollies vary considerably in shape and size throughout Britain, depending on their county of origin, and are called names such as 'The Pickering Chalice', 'The Essex Terret' and 'The Durham Chandelier'.

The five-straw plait is one of the easiest ways to start a dolly. It forms the core of a number of more intricate variations which you can then go on to try.

Obtaining the straw

If you live in the country you may have wheatfields nearby. Not all wheats are suitable, however, as only those varieties having hollow straws such as Elite Lepeuple and Maris Widgeon can be used. If you find a farmer who is growing the right wheat he may be kind enough to let you cut some of the straw when nearly ripe. If you are unable to get real straw, you can buy artificial straws in craft shops.

Storing

To prevent your straw getting mildew it must first be allowed to dry out. Do this by laying it in the sun or in an airing cupboard, spread on paper.

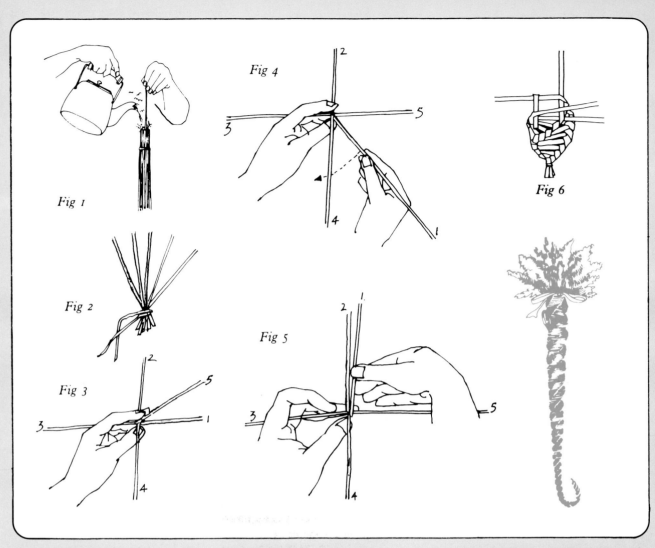

Fig 1

Fig 2

Fig 3

Fig 4

Fig 5

Fig 6

Trimming

Cut each straw just above the stem joint below the ear, and just above the bottom joint at the base. Remove the leaf that grows from the bottom joint.

Grading

Your straw will probably be of varying shapes and sizes, so sort it into bundles of fine, medium and thick.

Preparation

Artificial straw does not need dampening, but if you are using real straw you must dampen it to keep it pliable. Take a bundle of straws and secure the thick ends with a rubber band. Pull one of the straws a little way out from the rest, and using this to hold the bundle, pour hot water over the rest (fig 1).

Five-Straw Plait

The five-straw plait is the basis of many different corn dollies. Practise using paper drinking straws before starting to work with real straw.

a) Tie five straws together at the ends with a clove-hitch using strong linen thread (fig 2).

b) Holding the tied ends in your left hand, bend four of the straws down at right angles. Bend the fifth straw right on top of straw 1 (fig 3).

c) Bend straw 1 under straw 5 and over to straw 4 (fig 4).

d) Bend straw 1 up and over straw 5 tightly to lie beside straw 2 (fig 5).

e) Holding straws 1 and 2 together with your right hand, release your grip with your left hand and turn the straws clockwise to what is now the new starting position. Repeat the instructions from a) but this time using straw 2, then straw 3. Use each straw in turn, until you feel confident about making the five-straw plait.

The size of the spiral you make depends on the way you work the straws. To increase the spiral, put the 'moving' straw to the right of the straw it bends over.

If you want your corn dolly to be a uniform shape, it helps if you work round an object such as a pencil.

To add straws, simply push the end of the new straw into the end of the old one and carry on working. To finish off, tuck the ends of the straws back down inside the spiral, or tie thread tightly round the ends and cut them off neatly. For a final touch you can tie a piece of ribbon round the dolly to hang it up with.

SWIMMING

photographs by Tony Rose

Lord Baden-Powell believed that everybody should learn to swim, and most people would agree that it is important to learn to swim while you are young. Swimming is a wonderful way to exercise as it involves the whole body. Almost anyone can enjoy it, from the very young to the elderly, from the very fit to the physically disabled. This is because water has the property of being able to support the body on or near its surface. This takes the strain off the muscles which normally keep us erect, allowing more freedom of movement.

Floating

People float in different ways depending on the density of their body tissue. Most find the air in their lungs keeps the upper part of their body buoyant, while their legs tend to sink.

Salt water is more dense than fresh water and easier to float in. The Dead Sea is so salty that you float like a cork and find it almost impossible to swim!

Different strokes

Front crawl or freestyle

When freestyle races were first introduced swimmers could choose their stroke, as the term freestyle implies, but with front crawl being the fastest way to move through the water competitors inevitably chose that stroke. Nowadays freestyle is virtually synonymous with front crawl. To swim front crawl well you need to keep your face in the water, except when breathing in of course! This keeps your body streamlined and allows the arms to circle properly.

Breast stroke

This is the oldest of the main swimming strokes and depends on a good leg kick to be effective. During a breast stroke race the swimmers must keep their heads above the water all the time or they can be disqualified.

These Guides from the 2nd and 3rd Goddington Companies are keen swimmers.

Butterfly

This is the most recent stroke to appear and is a development of the breast stroke. It was first used competitively after the 1952 Olympic Games.

Back stroke

Popular with beginners, back stroke enables you to swim quickly but to keep your face out of the water.

Side stroke

Another old stroke that was not considered a proper stroke, side stroke has recently become respectable as people recognise safety and survival as the prime aims of swimming. It is a leisurely way to swim for the not particularly strong or energetic, and easy for beginners.

Life-saving back stroke

This way of swimming shouldn't be thought of as the only method of life-saving. Side stroke can also be used when you're towing someone. Life-saving back stroke is a relaxing way to swim when you are tired.

Diving

There are a few safety rules that should always be observed when you want to dive:

- Never dive vertically into shallow water, that is water less deep than your height on tiptoe with your arms stretched above your head.
- Open your eyes under the water and keep them open until you surface, otherwise you may hit something or somebody.
- Keep your arms extended above your head with your hands together to protect your head from hitting the bottom of the pool or a stray swimmer at speed.
- Never swim in the diving area of the pool.

Practising life-saving.

Swimming safely

There are two aspects to water safety.

1 You should know how dangerous large expanses of water can be. To a toddler, a garden pond is a large expanse of water.

Never run along the side of the pool. It will be wet and may be slippery.

Never keep anyone under water. They may not be able to hold their breath as long as you, and could be in difficulties without you realising.

Never swim in the diving area of the pool when the boards are in use. A diver enters the water very fast, and if you are underneath you will come off worst.

Never throw anyone in from the side of the pool. You or they could easily overbalance or slip, and maybe hit the side of the pool.

Never swim in a river, lake, canal or the sea without supervision. Always have one person out of the water watching, ready to raise the alarm if anyone looks to be in difficulties. If there are several of you, pair up and each keep an eye on your partner.

Never swim straight after a meal or you may get cramp. Always wait at least an hour before going in. Don't swim if you are tired.

Never swim in the sea if there is a red flag flying. Check the tides and local currents and always obey the coastguard warnings.

2 You should know what to do in a crisis. Drowning accidents happen very suddenly. Be aware of the dangers, as you may be in a position to help. These are the principles to remember:

Observation

It's no good knowing how to rescue someone if you don't notice that they're in difficulties in the first place! Keep your eyes open for anyone who you know to be a poor swimmer, and also watch for children who may be playing about and get into dieep water.

Assessment

Any action you are going to take must be based on your own capabilities, without endangering yourself. So you must decide quickly whether to attempt a rescue yourself or whether to get help. If you are at a pool alert the lifeguard.

Action

Once you have assessed the situation and decided what to do, do it!

- If you are going to attempt to rescue the victim yourself, first try to reach them while remaining on dry land. Hold on to something secure so you don't fall in too. You can extend your reach using a branch, rope, pole, or even an item of clothing.
- Throw anything that will provide buoyancy. A rubber ring, piece of wood, beach ball, any of these would do. Aim slightly to the side of the victim; it wouldn't help them to be knocked out by a chunk of wood!

- To help you reach or throw more accurately, you could wade out, but never go deeper than thigh depth. If you can, use a stick to feel in front of you for changes of depth.
- Swim only if you are a strong swimmer and know what you are doing. Take a buoyancy support with you. Remember the victim may be panicking so don't get too close. Use a towing aid, e.g. an article of clothing, if possible.
- If you think a rescue attempt would be risky, go for help at once.

The best way to prevent drowning accidents is for everyone to learn to swim. If you don't have swimming lessons at school, find out whether your local pool runs classes in the evening. If you can swim, try to encourage any friends who can't to go along to the pool for lessons. Show them what fun swimming is and they'll soon want to join in!

Perhaps one day, if you train hard, and make all the special preparations, you will be allowed to try a Channel swim, like the group of five Guides and one Ranger who swam from Cape Griz Nez in France to Lydden Spout near Folkestone in 1966, achieving a new record for a team of girl swimmers!

We're hav...

All parties are fun – but a special party is even better! Make yours special with a theme!

Have a glittering party! Everything has to sparkle. Get out your Christmas decorations, string up the fairy lights. Wear glitter sprayed on your hair and dusted on your cheeks and shoulders. Tie your hair with tinsel and wear a silver ribbon round your neck. Blow up balloons, paint on shapes with glue and sprinkle on glitter powder – make invitations the same way on silver card. Stick silver doyleys on the windows. Serve sparkling lemonade in silver paper cups.

Come to a party

Have a pop star party! Everyone bri... poster of the... favourite star a... record... the pos... dance...

Have a swimming... Choose a fairly quie... time and go along t... your local pool. Have coffee and cakes afterwards in the café.

Have a fish 'n' chip party! No need to dress up for this one – just comfortable clothes, coke and records – halfway through the evening, send out for fish 'n' chips!

...g a party!

Have a musical party!
Everyone brings an instrument – have a prize for the best musician and one for the worst! Play along with your records!

Have a fancy dress party with a difference!
Everyone must come as the same thing or person – a clown or a tramp or a witch, or all the girls as Toyah and all the boys as Shakin' Stevens, or girls as Aunt Sally and boys as Worzel Gummidge!

Have a garden party!
Choose a summer afternoon, spread a rug on the grass and wear a pretty dress (hats are optional!) Serve cucumber sandwiches and little cakes.

Or have a party with a colour theme! Turn over for ideas for a "Pink" party!

Think

Everyone must wear pink!
Have pink balloons and streamers, cut
shapes out of pink tissue paper and
stick them to the windows. Make bows
with cheap ribbon and tie them
over pictures and mirrors.
Replace the light bulbs with pink
tinted bulbs to create a rosy
glow over everything!

Wear pink shoes!
Make little tassels with pink wool
and sew them onto your ballet pumps.
Or make pom-poms for the heels of your
newly-
painted plimsolls. Sew
pom-poms onto pink
lurex laces as well!

Present a pretty pink image!
Wear pale pink sparkle on your
cheeks and glitter in your hair,
which is tied with pink ribbons
and flowers.
Sew tiny pink
flowers onto
a hairslide
or pony tail
band.

Serve a pretty pink "cocktail"
lemonade with a dash of
strawberry syrup, a
pink cocktail
parasol and
a pink straw.

PINK!

Buy 80 cm. of pink fabric (lurex would look great!) and make this tabard - just two rectangles of fabric with ribbon-ties at the shoulder, and sashed at the hip with a wide satin ribbon. Wear it over different shades of pink jumper, tights, leg-warmers and little pink pumps.

50 cm. (approx.)

80 cm.

Tie your tiny ponytail with a band to which you've added lengths of pink cord tipped with beads and feathers (from a feather duster!)

Serve pink food on pink paper plates and pink drinks out of pink paper cups. Have a bowl of taramasalata with some warmed pitta bread, make pink salmon pinwheel sandwiches. With a biscuit cutter, cut heart shapes from buttered white bread and sprinkle with hundreds and thousands. Bake cakes tinted pink with food colouring, make little pink cakes, turn them upside down and make little pink mice with red liquorice for a tail and silver balls for eyes and nose!

SAVE OUR SWANS

Photographs by Norman Redfern

Have you ever stopped to admire a beautiful swan peacefully gliding across water, its head held proudly above a snowy white back? I'm sure you will agree it is one of the loveliest sights, but unfortunately becoming all too rare as swans join the ever-growing list of wildlife in danger.

The main threat to swans comes from fishing tackle discarded by anglers. Fishing line becomes entangled around their feet and beaks, and hooks become embedded in their flesh or even swallowed. Tiny lead weights left by fishermen are picked up by swans as they graze, and as these accumulate in the swan's gizzard, it is poisoned. It is natural for swans to pick up small pieces of gravel to help their digestion — unfortunately the lead pellets are of a similar size. Unless fishermen can be persuaded to use non-toxic weights, more and more swans will die of lead-poisoning.

The problem is particularly acute in Norfolk, an area popular with both swans and anglers. The number of swans injured and dying on the Norfolk broads through the carelessness of fishermen prompted Len and Sheila Baker to set up the Norfolk Swan Rescue Service. Since the service began over 1000 swans have been rescued although not all have recovered from their injuries. Many are too badly hurt or poisoned to save, and all Len and Sheila can do is make their last few hours more comfortable. But, with the help of a friendly vet and using equipment paid for by donations, over five hundred swans have been saved. Ninety per cent of the injuries are from fishing tackle or lead poisoning.

When Len and Sheila hear of a sick or injured swan, they or a couple of the other helpers go to the rescue. They have two rubber dinghies with outboard motors and a swan 'ambulance' with a radio telephone for emergencies.

If more anglers were aware of the problem and took every bit of tackle home, the swans could live in peace.

Volunteers help to clear ponds and clean out pens, and care for those swans who are recovering. A large caravan in the Bakers' garden is used as a hospital and treatment centre.

You can help the swans by making more people aware of the injuries that discarded fishing tackle can cause. If you go out walking along a river bank or beside a lake, take a carrier bag and pick up any litter, including fishing line (be very careful if you find any hooks), and put it in the dustbin as soon as you get home.

You can contact the Swan Rescue Service and find out other ways to help at Hill Farm House, The Street, Sparham, Norwich NR9 5PP, telephone (036 288) 460. The 24 hour rescue number for emergencies is (0603) 29444. The service relies on donations, not only of money, but also old blankets, sheets and towels, feeding bowls, bandages and adhesive tapes.

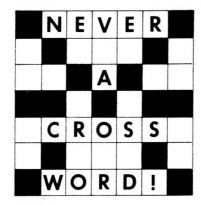

NEVER A CROSS WORD!

by Phil Stuart

Anyone who reads a daily newspaper will be familiar with that grid of squares beside a list of numbered clues, known as the crossword. In fact it's probably fair to say that few readers can resist the temptation of trying to solve those annoying clues, either giving up in frustration or emerging triumphant having beaten the compositor of the puzzle. There is something about a crossword that, once started, compels you to try and finish it. Picture if you can the state of the poor reader who is left with just one clue they cannot solve, only to find out when the solution is published that they knew the answer all along!

The first crossword appeared in December 1913 in the *New York World* newspaper. It was devised by a Liverpudlian named Arthur Wynne, who took the already popular word square (which contained words reading the same down and across) and developed it a stage further by providing a set of clues for both the down and across words, which had to be fitted into the grid. He used a diamond-shaped grid for the first puzzle, and it proved a massive success, becoming a regular feature in that and many other papers.

The first crossword to appear in a British newspaper was another of Arthur Wynne's puzzles, printed in an edition of the *Sunday Express* in 1924. By this stage the square format was being used.

It was in January 1924 that the idea of a book of crossword puzzles was formed. Richard Simon and Lincoln Schuster, who'd newly formed a publishing company, were responsible. An aunt of Simon's wanted to give a book of crossword puzzles as a present and asked where she might buy one. Simon and Schuster realised there was no such thing available and so published one. Edited by crossword experts of the *New York World*, it cost $1.35, and was a huge success.

Since then crosswords have grown and grown in popularity, but not without some strange events along the way. It seems that once bitten by the crossword bug, it can be very hard to break the habit, and in at least once case it has proved fatal! One evening a New York man asked his wife to help him solve a crossword. She refused and went to lie down, complaining that she was tired. Minutes later her husband burst into the bedroom brandishing a pistol and narrowly missed shooting her. She fled, but on hearing another shot returned to find her husband lying beside the unsolved puzzle.

Another strange story is about the Reverend George McElveen, who produced a crossword in front of his congregation and refused to preach until it had been solved. When the congregation finally solved it, they found the crossword contained the text of his intended sermon!

There have been many different shapes and forms of crossword. One man compiled a huge three-dimensional puzzle, with 3375 cubes. It took him two years to compile and had three types of clues – across, down and through!

Whichever form crosswords take, from triangular to three-dimensional, from mini to giant, from easy to cryptic, solving them has proved one of the most popular leisure activities in the world, and will continue to do so for years to come.

Answers to Scrambled Badges

Air Hostess	Crewing
Archery	Explorer
Artist	Flower Arranger
Astronomer	Home Management
Ballroom Dancer	Motor Mechanic
Drama	Skin Diver
Boatswain	Shipwright
Campcraft	Space Travel

HOLD THE FRONT PAGE!

Have you ever realised that you don't need to be famous to appear in a newspaper? You could make your own, featuring your family and neighbours or your Guide Company.

You will need: some large sheets of plain paper, ballpoint and felt pens, a stapler.

First of all, fold the sheets of paper in half like a newspaper and staple them at the fold.

Your newspaper now needs a name – you could call it *Guide Mail* or *News from My World,* anything you like. As you will have noticed from the newspapers around your house, the front page always has a headline printed in large letters. This has to catch the public's eye to make them want to read more. You may want to tell your readers how your brother James had an accident on his bicycle. Describe underneath the headline how the accident happened, what type of bike he owns, whether he or the bicycle were damaged and perhaps make a few suggestions as to how the accident could have been avoided, warning your readers of the dangers of riding a bicycle improperly.

Newspapers generally include photographs. You could draw pictures, illustrating your front-page story and the features inside the paper. Unlike most newspapers yours can be in colour, to make the paper really come to life. You may even have some old photos to spare which can be stuck on the page or fixed with photograph corners.

Inside there could be a fashion page, describing a new outfit, or interviews with various people to find out their views on school uniform or their ideas for future fashions.

One section could be devoted to Badges which the Guides in your Company have gained; you could make it look like the column for births and marriages in the papers. Or describe your Company's most recent fund-raising efforts.

Maybe you have tried out a new recipe recently and could write it out in your 'cookery section'. Any recent films or television programmes you have seen could be reviewed. Outline the story briefly, and say what you liked (or didn't like) about it. Don't give the ending away if you decide to review a film; it may spoil it for your friends if they haven't seen it.

You will find many more ideas by looking through old newspapers at home. The most important things are to write clearly and make it as interesting as you can. Who knows, maybe you will be asked to write one every week.

Debbi Scholes

STOP PRESS STOP PRESS STOP PRESS STOP PRESS STOP PRESS STOP PRESS STOP PRESS S

How would you like to see one of our national daily newspapers 'put to bed'?

That is the prize for the lucky winners in our exciting competition. To enter, you must write a report of 200-300 words suitable for a magazine or newspaper either about some Guide event you have attended (a Guide Meeting will do), or about somebody who is or was in the Guide Movement – perhaps your Gran remembers being a Guide, or maybe your District Commissioner is willing to be interviewed?

The writers of the best reports in each category will be invited to spend an evening at the offices of the DAILY MIRROR, watching the paper being prepared with the next day's news. Travelling expenses for each winner plus a relative will be paid, and overnight accommodation can be provided as the trip will finish late – papers sometimes don't go to bed before midnight!

Send your entry to:
The Editor, Girl Guide Annual,
17–19 Buckingham Palace Road,
London SW1W 0PT

Don't forget to include your name, address, age and Guide Company, and also tell us the three items you liked best in this annual. This is most important as it helps us to know what to put in the next one.

The closing date of the competition is March 31st, 1984. Winners will be notified by post and the Editor's decision is final.

—they rowed down the dark stream

ART'S QUIZ

by Cecilia Fellner

1. Who sang that all she wanted was a room somewhere?
2. What animal is Comrade Napoleon in *Animal Farm*?
3. Which sport did Miss Jo Hunter Dunn play so splendidly?
4. Who wrote the words and music of our National Anthem?
5. Who wrote *Land of Hope and Glory*?
6. What do we call West Indian popular music?
7. Who does Laurie eventually marry in *Good Wives*?
8. Who says and in what play: 'He is the very pineapple of politeness'?
9. Who wrote a 'surprise' symphony and why?
10. Why did Tweedledum and Tweedledee agree to have a battle?
11. Who wrote the story of Bernard and Ethel when she was only nine?
12. What are Jellicles and who named them in his book of poems?
13. What were the 'real' names of the following:
    a) The Scarlet Pimpernel
    b) The Barber of Seville
    c) The Lost Boys
    d) The Merchant of Venice
    e) The Waltz King
    f) The Hunchback of Notre Dame
    g) 007?
14. Was Shakespeare born on:
    a) Mothering Sunday, or
    b) St George's Day, or
    c) August Bank Holiday?
15. Who is this famous actor and what role is he playing?

drawing by Lorraine Deller

Answers on page 62

DOING A STRETCH!

by Selina Still

illustrated by Hilary Mullock

Try these simple exercises to keep yourself fit and supple.
Before you begin, remember these points:

- **Wear loose, comfortable clothing. A leotard, or shorts and a T-shirt are best.**
- **Don't do them after a heavy meal; wait a couple of hours first.**
- **Use a rug to work on, or an old blanket folded in half.**
- **Try to work in a room with open windows, so you can breathe fresh air.**

- **If it is fine go outside, but check with Mum or Dad that you can take the rug out with you.**
- **When following the instructions, try to keep to the breathing pattern, but don't hold your breath.**
- **Stretch — don't strain. When you are doing the exercises, don't try to reach too far. Do what is comfortable for you.**
- **Relax — don't collapse! When you have completed the exercise, return slowly to the starting position.**
- **Practice makes perfect. You will find it easier to keep supple if you exercise regularly.**

Begin with an exercise for the spine and back muscles

2 bend forward from the hips, breathing out slowly

3 look through your legs, breathing in and out slowly

1 stand straight

4 gradually straighten up breathing in as you rise

60

This next exercise is also good for the back

1 stand straight, feet apart, hands on hips

2 take a deep breath then breathe out slowly as you bend to the right

3 breathe in as you come up, breathe out and bend to the left

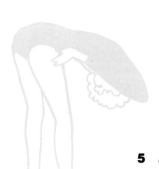

4 repeat, leaning backwards . . .

5 . . . and forwards

Now try this exercise

1 kneel on the floor with your arms straight down

2 breathe out and arch your back right up, like a cat

3 breathe in, curve your back down, bring your head right up

61

Try this one for the legs

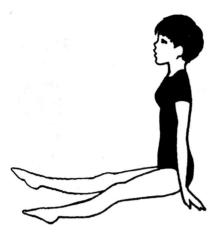  

1 sit on the floor with your back straight

2 put the soles of your feet together and bring your legs up

3 rock your knees up and down like a butterfly's wings

This exercise is good for the neck and shoulders

1 kneel on the floor

2 slowly breathe out and lower your head and shoulders to the floor

3 breathe in and go forward, keeping your head and shoulders parallel to the floor

4 breathe out, return to position 2, then breathe in and return to position 1

Answers to QUIZ on page 59

1. Eliza Doolittle.   2. A pig!
3. Lawn tennis.   4. No one knows – not even Buckingham Palace.   5. Sir Edward Elgar composed the music – the tune is in one of his military marches *Pomp and Circumstance*. A. C. Benson wrote the words.
6. Reggae. It has 4 beats to the bar with the upbeat strongly accented.   7. Amy, the youngest of the four March sisters.

8. Mrs Malaprop in Sheridan's *The Rivals*. By pineapple she meant pinnacle.   9. Haydn. At the end of a simple melody very quietly played, the whole orchestra suddenly produced a very loud sound. This was intended to awake anyone who had dozed off after a large meal!
10. 'Tweedledum said Tweedledee had spoiled his nice new rattle'.   11. Daisy Ashford. She wrote *The Young Visiters*, but

please don't copy her spelling. Illustration reproduced by kind permission of the Author's Literary Estate and Chatto & Windus Limited.   12. According to T.S. Eliot, they are black and white, not too big, roly-poly cats.   13. a Sir Percy Blakeney b Figaro c Barrie never tells us d Antonio e Johann Strauss f Quasimodo g James Bond.
14. b St George's Day.
15. Laurence Olivier as Hamlet.